MORE
THAN WEARING THE
UNIFORM

Balancing Military Life, Finances and Family

Written By

KHARYE J. POPE

Dedication

For every service member who is feeling
overwhelmed by the life they are living
You are not alone!

Table of Contents

CHAPTER 1

Military Life

W E ALL HAVE OUR REASONS for joining the military. Some people join because they want to get an education. Other's join because they are seeking economic opportunity. There are also those who join because they have a family legacy of serving. We all have our own motivations and have an idea of what it is going to be like during our period of service. Unfortunately, what we thought we had signed up for is not always what we actually experience.

As a young enlistee you may experience being away from home for the first time. You probably do not have a great deal of money. You are surrounded by people who are just as disoriented as you are, but may handle it a little bit better. You are still adjusting to being a member of the armed forces. You are introduced to the Uniform Code of Military Justice (UCMJ) and learn that there are a set of rules and regulations that require you conduct yourself in a certain manner. All of this takes time to adjust to.

Hopefully, you have someone at your command that you can turn to that will show you what to do. Unfortunately, a large number of junior enlisted personnel do not have this and are left to discover this on their own. An even worse scenario is turning to someone who gives you bad advice. The question is, how do you know you are receiving bad advice?

Take a good look at the individual who is advising you. Is this person someone who is respected within your work section/command? Is he or she in a leadership position entrusted with authority? Is the person knowledgeable in their job and professional in their conduct? If they are you should pay attention to what they say, and how they carry themselves. If they say something that doesn't seem right you should confirm what they are saying with someone else.

A problem that is common to all junior enlisted personnel (unless you have a rich relative/trust fund) is money, or more specifically, the lack of it. Most junior enlisted personnel do not have an opportunity to work a second job, or start a business while on active duty so for the most part, you have to work with what you have in terms of your pay.

The fact that you don't make much money is well known and there are entire industries dedicated to taking your money from you. Many of them are located right outside of your duty station's gates. They know that over the period of your service that you are going to get a paycheck. They also know that they can have your command attached through the military involuntary allotment process to ensure that you pay what you owe.

Involuntary Allotments

It is Department of Defense (DoD) policy that military members pay their just financial obligations in a proper and timely manner. Creditors who have been awarded a civil judgment against a military member may seek enforcement of the judgment by applying for an involuntary allotment from the member's military pay. Applications for involuntary allotments cannot be based on garnishments as active duty military are not subject to garnishment for commercial debts.

If approved, the allotment can pay up to a maximum of 25 percent of the member's disposable pay per monthly pay period. (Note: not all pay that a military member receives is subject to involuntary allotment). A creditor may initiate this process against a military member by submitting an Involuntary Allotment Application along with a certified copy of a final judgment issued by a civil court. A judge, not the clerk of the court, must sign the final judgment. Defense Finance and Accounting Service (DFAS) must be served with an original and two copies of both

he form and the judgment. Also, the application must contain the member's full name and social security number for positive identification.

Because the regulation mandates that military members be allowed
90 days notice before payments can begin, payments start 90 to 120 days
after we received the complete application. DFAS is the only authorized
agent for service of these applications for all branches of the military services (except the U.S. Coast Guard). With respect to interest, Post-judgment interest is payable under the regulation but it must be awarded
in the judgment. Creditors who submit judgments from jurisdictions
where post-judgment interest is statutory should submit copies of the
statute that authorizes the interest along with their application.

Keep in mind that the maximum amount that may be withheld from
individual's pay to satisfy commercial debts is 25 percent of the individual's disposable pay. Disposable pay is the gross pay minus certain
authorized deductions, such as income tax withholding or debts owed
to the government.

Predatory Service Providers

You see the advertisements that blanket military communities offering
military personnel instant approval on whatever product that is being
sold regardless of credit. Let's say you finance a brand new MacBook,
some furniture and a few home appliances for a low weekly/monthly
payment. The retail value for what you are buying may be $4,500. But
by the time you finish paying for what you have bought with all of the
interest and fees you will have paid $13,000.

One of the worst offenders was retail chain USA Discounters, a
privately held company based in Norfolk, Virginia home of the largest
Naval Base in the world (Naval Station Norfolk). The Consumer
Financial Protection Bureau (CFPB) ended a service member fee scam
where USA Discounters tricked thousands of service members into
paying fees for legal protection service members **already have** (see the

Servicemembers Civil Relief Act (SCRA) below) and for services that the company failed to provide.

History of the Servicemembers Civil Relief Act (SCRA)

Recognizing the special burdens that members of the military may encounter trying to meet their financial obligations while serving their country, in 1940 Congress passed the Soldiers' and Sailors' Civil Relief Act (SSCRA). The law was amended from time to time, ordinarily in response to military operations that required the activation of the Reserves. P.L. 108-189, the Servicemembers Civil Relief Act (SCRA), was enacted on December 19, 2003, as a modernization and restatement of the protections contained in the SSCRA.

Much like with the SSCRA, the SCRA has been amended since its initial passage and proposed changes continue to be introduced in Congress. This report summarizes the rights granted to persons serving on active duty in the U.S. Armed Forces, and in some instances, to their dependents, under the SCRA.

The SCRA provides protections for servicemembers in the event that their military service impedes their ability to meet financial obligations incurred before entry into active military service. Forgiving of all debts or the extinguishment of contractual obligations on behalf of servicemembers who have been called up for active duty is not required, nor is absolute immunity from civil lawsuits provided.

Instead, the act suspends civil claims against servicemembers and protects them from default judgments. The SCRA includes provisions that prohibit the eviction of military members and their dependents from rental or mortgaged property; create a cap on interest at 6% on debts incurred prior to an individual entering active duty military service; protect against the cancellation of life insurance or the non-reinstatement of health insurance policies; allow some professionals to suspend malpractice or liability insurance while on active duty; and proscribe taxation in multiple jurisdictions and forced property sales in order to pay overdue taxes.

The U.S. Attorney General is authorized to commence a civil action to enforce provisions of the SCRA. Additionally, servicemembers and their dependents have the right to commence a civil action, that is, a private cause of action, to enforce protections afforded them under the SCRA.

The Servicemembers Civil Relief Act (SCRA)

Signed into law in 2003, the Servicemember's Civil Relief Act (SCRA) expanded and improved the former Soldiers' and Sailors' Civil Relief Act (SSCRA). The SCRA provides a wide range of protection for individuals entering, called to active duty in the military, or deployed servicemembers. It is intended to postpone or suspend certain civil obligations to enable service members to devote full attention to duty and relieve stress on the family members of those deployed servicemembers. A few examples of such obligations you may be protected against are:

- Outstanding credit card debt
- Mortgage payments
- Pending trials
- Taxes
- Termination of leases

In addition, the new law:

- Expands current law that protects servicemembers and their families from eviction from their housing while on active duty due to nonpayment of rent that is $3,329.84 per month or less for 2015 and this amount changes every year.
- Provides a servicemember who receives a permanent change of station orders or who is deployed to a new location for 90 days or more the right to terminate a housing lease.
- Clarifies and restates the existing law that enforces a limit of 6 percent interest on credit obligations incurred prior to military

service or activation, including credit card debt, for active duty service members. The SCRA unambiguously states that no interest above 6 percent can accrue for credit obligations (that were established prior to active duty or activation) while on active duty, nor can the excess interest become due once the service-member leaves active duty. Instead that portion above 6 percent is permanently forgiven. Furthermore, the monthly payment must be reduced by the amount of interest saved during the covered period. Note: This law only covers debt incurred prior to military service.

- Allows you to terminate a cell phone contract if you relocate for at least 90 days to a location that does not support your cell phone service.
- Allows you to terminate a vehicle lease you signed prior to joining the armed forces if you enter military service under a call to duty on orders of 180 days or more. You may also terminate a vehicle lease if you receive PCS orders to an OCONUS location or deploy OCONUS for at least 180 days.

SCRA Eligibility

The SCRA covers all active duty service members, reservists and the members of the National Guard while on active duty. The protection begins on the date of entering active duty and generally terminates within 30 to 90 days after the date of discharge from active duty.

The CPFB found that USA Discounters harmed service members with unfair and deceptive acts and practices including:

- Deceptively marketing its own legal obligation as a service to service members
- Misleading service members into believing they would have an independent representative
- Failing to provide actual services to struggling borrowers

See – www.consumerfinance.gov/newsroom/cfpb-shuts-down-usa-dis-counters-servicemember-fee-scam

In part due to their exploitive behavior being exposed, USA Discounters has filed for bankruptcy protection (Chapter 11). Unfortunately, USA Discounters is not the only bad actor out there. Every command has a list of companies and/or service providers that service members are advised to stay away from. Among these include but are not limited to:

- Payday Loans
- Title Loans
- Buy Here – Pay Here Car Lots (New or Used)

There is nothing wrong with purchasing what you really need, just be certain that you are doing business with a company that provides products you need at a reasonable price. Discussing your plans for major purchases with someone at your command who does not have a conflict of interest is good. Bring someone from your command with you to watch your back is even better. Don't allow a pretty face in a short skirt cost you thousands of dollars.

CHAPTER 2

Deployment

IN 1832, CARL VON CLAUSEWITZ said "War is a continuation of politics by other means..." We have an increasing number of politicians who have never served and have no personal connection to anyone who has served. Their lack of personal connection to those who have worn the uniform makes it easier for them to deploy service members to war because they are disconnected from the result of that decision.

Fast forward to today where the tradition of fighting wars continues. The United States has ended Operation Iraqi Freedom (OIF) after a ten-year period of conflict and the still continuing Operation Enduring Freedom (OEF) in Afghanistan – where combat operations drew to a close on December 28, 2014. We are moving closer and closer to becoming more involved in Syria and in combating the Islamic State of Iraq and the Levant (ISIL).

The service members fighting in these wars are emotionally worn and physically battered; but these men and women know that they have to do their job because other people's lives depend upon them doing so. They know that by doing their job, they keep each other safe and earn the right to return home to the people they love.

Military service requires service members to spend a significant amount of time away from home. The result of this absence is a tremendous strain on military families which causes the dissolution of marriages for some servicemembers. The military is consistently regarded as the institution Americans have the most respect for and its importance is unparalleled in the United States. Serving in the military impacts families greatly and the stress from that service contributes to the divorce rate among servicemembers.

When the decision is made to serve in the military, servicemembers are agreeing to give their body and spirit to defending this country. The oath of enlistment taken by all enlisted personnel states "I, 'state your name' do solemnly swear (or affirm) that I will support and defend the Constitution of the United States against all enemies, foreign and domestic; that I will bear true faith and allegiance to the same; and that I will obey the orders of the President of the United States and the orders of the officers appointed over me, according to the regulations and the Uniform Code of Military Justice. So help me God." (Title 10, US Code).

No one made you take that oath. This is something that you chose to do and as such, you have to live with the consequences of the choice. The consequences of the choice have an impact on you as well as your family. By signing that contract, you are committing your heart, body and soul. The only thing that is constant with military life is the fact that you will be moving.

As operational tempo increases and the size of the force remains the same size or gets smaller, it guarantees that you will be moving. You may be moving stateside for training or you may be deployed overseas. Regardless of where you find yourself sent to, every service member will spend an extended period of time away from their home, their family and their friends. Training and Deployment require that service members are often away from home for weeks if not months at a time.

Standard deployment lengths and frequency have increased and show no signs of decreasing. This has introduced a degree of uncertainty and stress that can be toxic for a relationship in it's developmental stages. Relationships end while the service member and their spouse are separated for extended periods of time such as deployments. Defense Department statistics indicate that the divorce rate among officers and enlisted personnel over 2014 was 3.1% which is lower than a high of 3.7% in 2011.

Expert Article:
Giving a Boost to Military Marriages

As if it isn't enough that soldiers risk their lives from our country, they also risk their marriages due to long separations and the stress that accompanies active military service. I've had requests from some service members for tips on keeping the home fires burning, as well as how to effectively reunite the family after a tour of duty. Thankfully, two in-depth interviews with exemplary military families helped shed some light on this topic. Any families enduring a long separation could use some of these tips.

Before the Soldier Leaves:

- Enlist the help of family, friends, church members and neighbors to help support the family while the soldier is away. Make a list of concrete ways your family will need help, from lawn or home maintenance to babysitting or grocery shopping.
- The spouse at home may need to learn to accept help, even when he or she hasn't in the past. It helps to focus on the support and love rather on the negative circumstances of being separated from the spouse.
- Invite letters, care packages and prayers and provide simple guidelines that would be helpful for the soldier or unit.
- Give the immediate family plenty of alone time prior to the deployment.

While the Soldier is away:

- Consider a blog to help keep family and friends updated on your own schedule. This prevents having to repeat updates on the soldier or unit (for the soldier and spouse at home) and keeps the soldier updated on the family.

- Remember phone calls can be inconvenient for one or both spouses. Plan a convenient time if phone calls are important.
- Play upbeat, fun music to keep the house from getting somber. Plan fun activities with friends or family.
- Use videoconferencing only if it makes sense for your family. For some spouses it is too painful. For young children, they may not understand why mommy or daddy is on the screen, but they can't touch them.
- Focus on the positive aspects of your spouse and your life. Keep negative news at bay by turning off the news and keeping TVs out of the bedrooms.
- Keep precious reminders of loved ones close at hand-a special letter, a photo of each family member, perhaps a special piece of jewelry or memento.
- The traveling spouse may still be able to handle certain home responsibilities, such as banking, with online services.
- Young children who don't have a concrete understanding of time could make a paper chain with a link for each day the soldier will be away. Invite them to send pictures and letters to their absent parent.
- Reach out to support groups or other spouses in similar circumstances.

When the Soldier Returns:

- Plan a welcome-home celebration to thank everyone who has offered support and to honor the soldier for his or her service.
- Be patient. Particularly when the soldier has been gone for a lengthy tour, the family has often adapted to his or her absence, and the soldier may no longer feel as if he or she fits in as before.

The at-home spouse became the leader and took the role of two parents, so time to assimilate is needed. Give the immediate family space and time to sort this out. Children may also need time to sort through their emotions.

- Be sensitive to soldier's sleep needs. The soldier has just returned from a different world and may be battling anxiety, nightmares, difficult sleep patterns or may awaken disoriented after having just returned.
- Express your gratitude and praise to the spouse who cared for the family as well as to the soldier who performed in the field.
- Stress can often bring a couple closer together. Use the experience as a catalyst for recognizing and appreciating what is truly important to you both.

Two in-depth military profiles will be shared in my upcoming book, *From First Kiss to Lasting Bliss, Secrets of Successful Marriages*. Contact me if you would like to stay updated on the book's progress. Special thanks to all members of the military, single and married.

Lori Lowe is a writer and communications consultant from Indianapolis. Her blog www.lorilowe.wordpress.com encourages couples in their marriages and family relationships. Subscribe today to read a positive voice in your inbox. Lori is currently researching and writing a book profiling couples who have overcome significant obstacles and who have insightful lessons to share.

Article Source: EzineArticles.com/expert/Lori_Lowe/133722
Article Source: EzineArticles.com/2557338

CHAPTER 3

Challenges of Marriage in the Military

IT HAS BEEN SUGGESTED THAT the increased divorce rate could be due to troop withdrawals from Iraq and Afghanistan. When family members are separated for an extended period of time, they are not used to each other when they are reunited. This could lead to conflict within the household.

There are many reasons for divorce and they cannot simply be blamed on one factor. Early in your career you may not have much life experience. We have all had the experience of meeting someone and allowing our emotions to overrule our common sense. We feel strongly for someone and make decisions without taking the time to be certain that the person who we care for is actually who we think they are.

We make decisions without understanding what the costs are. Sometimes we are in love with an ideal and not the reality. As an example, say a junior enlisted service member meets someone and they have been together for a short period of time. The service member has never felt like this about anyone before and the object of the service member's affection feels the same way. They make the decision to get married believing they will live happily ever after.

Unfortunately, this is not what happens. The newly married couple does not know each other nearly as well as they thought. The service member is works long hours preparing for an exercise and the life that the military spouse thought they were going to have is not the life they are living. The service member receives orders and the couple moves to a base in a remote part of the country where the military spouse doesn't know anyone.

The problems that were hidden below the surface of the relationship begin to surface and a child is on the way. Bitterness and resentment grow as the service member and the military spouse feel like they were deceived as neither party is the person that each one believed the other to be. Both parties realize they made a mistake, but they have a child to consider and want the child to be raised by both parents. Much of this could have been avoided if the service member and the military spouse spent more time getting to know one another before getting married.

There are those who argue that the military's marriage incentives may be the problem. On-base housing is not only based on pay-grade, but marital status as well. Married military members are assigned to better and more spacious housing in order to better accommodate a family. Along with better housing, the spouse of a military member is provided with all the benefits that the member receives (i.e. healthcare, commissary privileges, etc.)

This is thought to serve as an enticement to military members and their significant others to make a decision that is not well thought out. The service member and their significant other get married without being fully prepared just to take advantage of the benefits associated with being married. Unfortunately, many of these marriages abruptly come to an end due to failure to prepare for the future. When the spouse is deployed, an already struggling marriage will continue to fall apart and ultimately come to an end.

Expert Article:
How to Manage Stress When Your Military Partner Is Deployed To Active Duty

Military deployment can produce a great deal of stress and anxiety, not just on the servicemen and women who are called up to active duty, but on the people they leave behind, as well. Whether your spouse or loved one is leaving for the first time or for the nth time, emotional distress caused by military deployment is inevitable and has to be dealt with constructively.

Active duty comes with risk, danger, and unpredictability, and the stress and tension on military spouses and loved ones left behind is a regular part of every military connection. Don't let it get you down. You love that guy or girl who's going off to serve. Here are some tips to manage stress and anxiety while your partner is deployed, and keep your sanity until they are back in your arms again.

Communication is Key

The most important thing when your partner is deployed is keeping communication lines open between you.

Talk to each other as often as possible; having your partner on the other end of the line is the best way to say I love you, and to ease the pain caused by so many miles of separation and the emotional turmoil you are experiencing. Talking will keep you both connected. Hearing – and knowing – he or she is safe will keep your fear in check, and reassure both of you that life will return to normal before too long.

Your opportunity to communicate is limited, so steer clear of negative thoughts and pointless arguments. Be a straight shooter, talk about everyday things, and share your daily life with your partner.

Keep in mind that although you're distressed, your partner's situation is may be severe – he or she may be exposed to physical danger and other hardships of combat. Therefore, you need to be rock solid during this time. Instead of seeking emotional comfort, give it, along with encouragement and affirmations of your love. Doing this will give your partner the power to carry on and come home safely.

Being strong for your partner's sake has an added benefit: You will find that when you assume the role of an emotionally strong partner, internal strength becomes natural. It will grow within you, and you, too, will be able to carry on until you and your love are reunited.

There are now many resources and a variety of technologies that can help you stay in touch when you are separated by thousands of miles. These range from email to cell phones, Skype and video. Take advantage of all of these as they will help you greatly. As a personal suggestion, invest in a computer and webcam. And, get a good cell phone with a mobile video chat function. These will allow to receive communications from your partner any time. Military men and women do not keep regular working hours; so expect to chat on the fly wherever and whenever.

Seek Support

You don't have to go through tough times alone; seek assistance. There are many support groups for military spouses and partners; these exist for people to share feelings and experiences associated with a military lifestyle. Joining and actively participating in a military support group will bring you a great deal of relief. When you connect and share with people who truly understand how you feel, you gain an understanding of yourself and the inner strength that comes with it.

Consider talking to a professional counselor, if necessary. There's nothing wrong in seeking professional advice if you are finding it especially hard to cope. There are also other sources of support, such as family and friends.

Make Stress Management a Priority

There are also many effective stress management techniques. Experiment and find what works for you. Talk therapy with a professional, or even a friend, can be very helpful. You can also engage in spiritually empowering activities such as visualization exercises, yoga and prayer.

The important thing is to acknowledge your choice to be in a military relationship and accept that stress and anxiety during periods of deployment are part of the life you chose. Remember the person you fell in love with in the first place. The decision to overcome the challenge is yours, and your relationship definitely is worth it.

The Effect of Marital Strain on Deployed Service Members

Military divorces are generally devastating for both husband and wife. While the spouse is deployed to a combat zone, the last thing on their mind should be divorce papers. The psychological impact on deployed service members, is capable of creating dangerous situations in fire-fights and patrols. While being forward deployed in a combat zone, high morale is a necessity as troops must be ready and willing to fight. The prospect of a divorce creates a difficult situation where deployed service-members face depression in the wrong place and at the wrong time.

It is all too common to hear a service member saying, "I will be meeting my kid for the first time." With standard deployments extending to twelve months and due dates being nine months after conception, it happens more often than you think. It is critical that the expecting mother enrolls in Tricare and gets available help and support if she feels an emotional burden. It is equally critical that the wife keeps her deployed spouse updated when it comes to the baby. It will ease the mind of the deployed member, knowing that everything is going well at home.

After coming home from a long deployment, it can be hard for military members to take on an immediate father role. After seeing so much for so long, it can be hard to resume the life you had before deploying. Former Navy Seal, Chris Kyle, discussed the difficulties of coming home to a family consisting of a wife and children in his book, American Sniper. He discusses the difficulties associated with him taking on the role of a father while serving in the military.

After serving on multiple deployments that encompassed leaving his wife and kids, Chris Kyle wrote that he felt like he did not know his child on the same personal level as his wife. He had a problem connecting with a child that was essentially a stranger to him. The critical bonding that occurs between an infant and parents at birth was something that he was unable to experience which caused a distance he had difficulty closing. Because of this, it is critical that the servicemember eases their way into a father role.

Just as there are times when the father has difficulty connecting with the child, there are also circumstances where the child may not accept the father right away. This lack of acceptance can create tension within the family, as the father feels as if he is left out. The child's mother may feel angry by the fact that the father is trying to jump into a quick relationship with the child. The child's mother may feel anger that the father has not been there to support the mother and child for months. This anger and bitterness could add strain to the relationships.

One of the most difficult things a servicemember has to do is call home. In order to ease the minds of loved ones at home, service members often try to ensure that phone calls are always positive. The ability to compartmentalize the reality of being in a warzone and to still be able to call to the servicemembers mother on her birthday just days after one of his best friends was killed after receiving a gunshot wound in the neck and bleeding out. The ability to always tell his mother and family that he was doing great and everything was going well, when in reality, his morale of him and his fellow troops' morale was spiraling towards the ground.

Returning home from deployment is often difficult for many service members. The person that left is not the same person who is coming back. Having been tested in ways that are hard to express to someone who has not experienced the things they have, it can be hard to reintegrate into the life they had before being deployed. The amenities and convenience of a life untouched by combat seems surreal.

Service members are forced to adapt to the reality of their circumstances in order to cope with day to day life. Behaviors that would never be considered at home are common place and often necessary when forward deployed. Having been placed in such a high stressed environment for the duration of their tour, it is not something you can just turn off. You cannot just take off the uniform, put away your boots and act as if the last year to eighteen months did not happen.

Service members who return from being deployed still retain habits and behaviors practiced in the field. Returning service members are often overly aggressive drivers, are easily irritated, remain hyper-vigilant, and have difficulty sleeping having learned to function on much less than 8 hours of sleep a night. Sudden movements and loud noises cause service members to have heightened reflexes to react often before they realize it because our body's autonomic fight or flight response is heightened due to what they have experienced while being deployed. There is no quick fix for this. It is going to take time for the service member to adjust.

Expert Article:
Military Family: 5 Key Tips for Making the Deployment-To-Home Transition Smoother

Tip #1 – We all desire those first couple of months our spouse is home to be reminiscent of our honeymoon, even conjuring up a list of things to do as a couple or family. However, being overly eager to return to the pre-deployment normal can backfire. Too many commitments or activities can overwhelm the returning military spouse. Their life has been on a demanding and strict regime for many months prompting the need to decompress without unrealistic or unreasonable expectations.

When my husband returned home from deployments I avoided committing him to plans as a couple or a family for the first two or three weeks. I encouraged him to let me know when he was ready to re-engage with others and activities outside our home. Every family is different in what is sensible and wise, but the idea is to find what works best for the rhythm and needs of your family in order to achieve a doable transition.

Tip #2 – Lower Expectations – This can go both ways – for the spouse returning home and the spouse upholding the home. Having unreasonable expectations on each other can trigger added tension. Have you ever felt like things were out of sync with your spouse just after a homecoming? To a large degree this is normal. During deployments, growth happens. Deployments have inherent factors that develop and change us over time. This is especially true for your children. However, if this "out of sync" feeling persists, and doesn't get better with time, there's nothing wrong with counseling as a needed first step.

Tip #3 – <u>Don't Wait, Get Help</u> – Returning from a deployment can also mean new challenges. If unforeseen stress such as emotional or physical stress is present, it's vital to seek counseling and/or a medical professional. If you don't know where to start, contact your primary care physician or your nearest military family support center for programs targeted for meeting the unique needs of military couples and families. They are eager to support you. Taking action is doing the responsible thing for your family.

Tip #4 – <u>Control Celebratory Spending</u> – This may seem like a small matter, but most stress in a military family is over financial worries. After the long months of deployment are over, it is natural to want to celebrate your loved one's homecoming, but over celebrating by going out to much will wreak havoc in an already tight budget. Determine ahead of time a homecoming celebration budget. By sticking to a pre-determined celebration plan, you and your spouse will feel in control of your finances while at the same time keeping to your financial goals and celebrating responsibly.

Tip #5 – <u>Don't Rush Romance</u> – Depending on how well your deployment experience was, whether or not it went better than expected or worse then expected, don't rush intimacy. Even the smoothest deployments have their unique challenges, and this calls for caution. A couple that fosters patience and understanding creates a safe environment to express feelings or inadequacies. The key is to be tuned into your spouse and communicate. And intimacy will come when both of you are ready.

Deployments teach us many things about ourselves, our spouses, and our marriages. The ups and downs of the military lifestyle in general is one long transition with many revolutions. However, when we do some pre-planning and implement these 5 tips you can reduce the difficulty of the adjustment period.

From Lisa Nixon Phillips – the Retired Military Wife who passionately believes Faith Makes a Difference!

Article Source: EzineArticles.com/expert/Lisa_N_Phillips/1841310

CHAPTER 4

Post Traumatic Stress

POST-TRAUMATIC STRESS DISORDER IS A result of the culmination of traumatic events that occur in combat. Troops that are deployed to war zones are all too commonly returning back to the United States with post-traumatic stress disorder. In fact, 44% of veterans that have participated in Operation Iraqi Freedom or Operation Enduring Freedom claim that the re-entry in to civilian life was difficult, according to Rich Morin, author of, "The Difficult Transition from Military to Civilian Life."

When a military member returns home with post-traumatic stress disorder, life for both the service member and their family may become very difficult. A service member suffering from post-traumatic stress disorder will frequently be depressed. They will experience flashbacks and may have re-occurring nightmares. It is absolutely imperative that a troops spouse and children realize what the service member has gone through. Family members must provide support at all times.

Expert Article:
Post-Traumatic Stress – A Soldier and His Wife's Story

Anyone who has suffered traumatic events has "stress." And, by expanding the terminology of PTSD, I think of all my Emotional Freedom Technique (EFT) clients as having some form of "post-traumatic stress." And while military personnel have received the most attention in this regard, this is not exclusively a military problem. As an EFT practitioner, I work with the effects of past traumas with every client.

Traumatic events cause immediate disturbance in our energy system. The body downloads the trauma as in a cellular "jolt" or electrical shocks that ignite the sympathetic nervous system response. Without help with a release, this reflex will stay in the "on" position and cause a chain of aberrant emotional reactions, none of which involve inner peace or balance. As in postpartum depression, the severity of PTSD is dependent, to some extent, upon how much anxiety the person had before the traumatic event, perhaps explaining why some people are affected more than others. The more anxiety a person has internally, the less able they are to handle the overload.

This article is an example of how EFT rapidly and effectively helped one soldier and his wife, Nolan and Julia. They were already in the system for PSTD treatments but without the results they had hoped for. Julia took the initiative to find a better solution for their problems, off base. She had heard about how EFT was being used to help war veterans, and without even knowing where to begin, she Googled "EFT El Paso" and found my name.

In my opinion, this initial step of seeking help outside the base is, in itself, empowering. By removing one's self from the "cattle herd mentality" (Nolan's own words), it served to put some self-control back into their lives. Everyone has that choice. You can stay in one place and tread water, or you can find your own life preserver. In other words, "If what you're doing isn't working, do something else."

Nolan is a 35-year-old soldier, has been in the army for seven years, and had three combat deployments. Not long after returning from his third deployment to Iraq, Nolan checked himself into the William Beaumont Hospital for severe anxiety, having the feeling of wanting to "walk away from everything." With thoughts of going AWOL from the army and his own family, he rationalized they would do better without him because he felt like a failure. He was admitted for "passive suicidal thoughts" and spent nine days on medications for insomnia, anxiety, depression, and art therapy to "express his emotions," all with no result. In fact, by his estimation, the anxiety medications "really, really freaked me out" by intensifying colors and lights. Nolan also said he lived his daily life like he was still deployed, always on alert. He couldn't get close to or trust anyone, including his wife, and expected her to leave him eventually. The thought of yet another deployment was overwhelming.

When Nolan and Julia came to my office, they had viewed a You-Tube EFT demonstration, but never saw it used in person by an experienced practitioner. Nolan was quiet, inexpressive. After my grand EFT explanation, sat through his first tapping round only to say that it looked silly and was "just another bunch of crap." We addressed those beliefs next because it is strange looking and different from anything he'd been exposed to before. It is also a very important component during a treatment to express any internal resistance that stands in the way of the real healing work. After one tapping round of "this looks like a bunch of crap," he felt more relaxed, and it was easier to get through his prepared list of specific events. I had asked, during the initial phone consult for him, to prepare a list of bothersome memories to work on.

Even though he had been having problems falling asleep and staying asleep for more than an hour at a time, Nolan informed me that he had run out of his sleep medications two days prior. I knew once we chiseled away at the big chunks, sleep would follow, so we did not tap directly on his sleep problem.

Some of his main issues were as follows:

- The highest priority on the list was the recurrent image of his fellow soldier, an acquaintance, laying dead with his brain hanging out of his head.
- Because the next events happened serially, I asked for the first time each specific event (bothersome memory) happened.
- The first time he had to kick in a door in Iraq. (He was a door kicker).

- The sound of the first mortar fly-over.
- The sight and sound of the first mortar hit. (Loud noises made him agitated and angry.)
- Anger about feeling used, just following orders as a door kicker, and putting his life on the line. (Nobody cares). Note: see why later.
- The first visual memory of deplaning in Iraq, and the fear levels when he thinks of it now.

I thought it was a highly productive session, ending with Nolan feeling sleepy, a common physical relaxation response, and a good indication of issues being cleared.

On their ride home from my office, his wife noticed that his demeanor had changed and his face took on an appearance of complete relaxation, as if he had just returned from a well needed vacation.

Once we cleared out the current traumatic events, childhood issues came to the forefront. He had unresolved childhood issues involving his mother, who was indifferent and unavailable, and who had eventually abandoned her whole family, i.e., "she didn't care," just as the Army "didn't care" what happened to him. We addressed those issues at our second hour-long session. As it often happens, getting the worst memories out of the way allows similar issues to generalize away very quickly. After working on the issues about his mother, trust in his wife came back to balance.

After two sessions of EFT, Nolan feels he is completely over his PTSD and his life overall has improved tremendously. In his own words, here is his progress report.

"The image of my fellow soldier who was shot and killed in Iraq, that I couldn't get out of my head, was completely gone after about 10 minutes of EFT. It's been a couple of weeks since our first session, and if I do think of him now, it's when he was alive and healthy."

"I didn't like the fact of how I felt the army had just used me being a door kicker; I was just following orders and putting my life out there. I've gotten over that anger as well."

"El Paso used to disturb me because some of the areas look like Iraq, but now, it's just El Paso, and we didn't even cover that in our session, it's what put me in the hospital in the first place, I was always on alert-because of the visual reminder."

"I was on sleep medications and having a real hard time going to sleep and staying asleep, even while I was hospitalized. I stopped taking the medications altogether, and now I'm sleeping the whole night every night. It's really great sleeping better. I handle stress a lot better now, and I don't need any of my medications. I feel calmer, and haven't had any anxiety problems since."

*Note: Its important to note that by law I cannot and do not advise any of my clients to stop their medications, and always refer them to their medical doctors for supervision.

Nolan and Julia attended our EFT Level 1 workshop shortly after his second session. Although she went there to support Nolan, during that time Julia discovered the roots of her own issues, and why Nolan's issues pressed so many buttons inside of her. One of them was the look on his face when he was heavily medicated. As a gift to all our attendees, we offer them a free half hour session with me as a jump-start on their own Personal Peace Procedure.

Julia, having had a close look at her husband's PTSD symptoms, was reminded of the daily traumatic stresses she endured as a child living with a heroin addict mother. Nolan's facial expressions, under the influence of psychotropic drugs was, to her, eerily similar to her moms when she was high. Highly resilient naturally, she had been suppressing her past throughout their marriage until the drugged face of her husband pushed an old button.

This is Julia's own testimonial after her half hour private session.

"I now feel like I'm more 'at one' with myself-more balanced, I don't feel so scattered. After the session, I went home and felt just like Nolan did when he left from his first session. I could see how relaxed he was, and for me, everything was just slower, like life just slowed down. I felt more content, and for the very first time in my whole world, I was able to start and finish a task.

At first, I was very reluctant to say anything to anyone because it almost seemed too quick and too good to be true! I was able to feel content, focus in on one thing at a time and finish it. And it happened again the very next day. By the third day, I was on the phone to my dad and telling him I had actually started and finished five different projects around my house, and it was a really good feeling."

In my world, I consider myself a leader, and I can "fake it" by assigning other people on the teams that I'm on to make up for my weaknesses, so I don't appear so scattered. At home, my own family knows that I'm all over the place and for the first time ever, I know what balance feels like."

"Internally, I've always had quite a bit of anger, and I can say now, those levels are now down to about a 3, I might even say a 1 or a 2, and I feel very relaxed and excited for my day. Overall, I feel very relaxed. It's been great!"

"I've had really bad attention problems. I couldn't finish anything and felt scattered and always overwhelmed. When we were at the EFT class, I was able to see more clearly how just much discontent I've always felt. My attention problems were so bad that I could never sit down with my husband and watch a movie-but I watched one the other day-very unusual!"

"I have never been able to wake up my three kids after infant/toddler age. It's been a huge issue that I don't feel like I was ever aware of until my husband's PTSD showed up, and they started medicating him, which caused flashes of old memories seeing the drugged look on his face. Sleep faces remind me of my mother who was a heroin addict. My father who raised me was a pothead. I grew up hating sleep because it meant that I was alone and isolated."

"My oldest child is 13 years old, and I have never been able to go to her room and wake her up seeing her sleepy. Once my children got to that age I would yell at them from a distance 'It's time to wake up!' If I didn't get immediate responses from them, and if they weren't lined up like soldiers at the top of the stairs at attention, then I was irritated, mad, and then yelling for having to wake them up myself. The hostility would surface, but I thought I was doing them a big favor by restraining my real anger. After my first session, I found the habit of standing at the top of the stairs to wake them still there, but the anger is completely gone."

"Before my first session and after the EFT workshop, I went all the way up the stairs just to test it. It took more time for me to get mad. With each step I could feel it building internally, I thought, 'I'm going to see the sleep face' and a few seconds later I could feel the hostility build.

After my private session, I told myself I'm going up there again, I did it, and I was fine. I was able to have a conversation with my daughter and had a zero intensity of anger. I was absolutely able to stand there and look at her groggy face! My daughter and I look just like my mother, it was unbelievable that I was able to stand there and have a conversation with her while she was waking up. Its sad to me that I used to get angry at my own daughter. In ten years I have never been able to see her wake up! This is huge progress! The only thing remaining is for me to get rid of the weird habit of going to the edge of the stairs."

"I never realized I hated looking at my kids sleeping-who says that? After this all unraveled with EFT I realized that my problems were very deep – I was really running from my mom's sleeping face, I've been running for years."

Specific events we worked on:

- I was afraid mom wouldn't wake up.
- I was alone when she nodded off.
- I felt betrayed each time she got high.
- Mom didn't love me.
- Mom didn't see me.
- Sleep means lazy.

Nolan and Julia now have EFT as a tool to handle the normal, ongoing stresses of life and to explore releasing long-held blocks to their happiness. They are part of a small but growing number of military PTSD victims who have taken the initiative to remove themselves from the rigidly conservative and ineffective approaches used by the Army.

The old guard has always resisted new approaches, and perhaps rightfully so since much that is "new" turns out to be of little use in the long run. Today's soldiers are in the unique position of purposely placing themselves in stressful situations. In many of these situations, they react to activities that are unnatural (freedom to kill humans and destroy property without corporal punishment). When they return home, they are expected to come back to "normal" and function "normally" again.

With almost 20 years of a track record in the treatment of stress-related conditions, EFT deserves more than a second look, it deserves to be recognized as a true "weapon" in the fight against PTSD. As essentially a self-help technique, it could be taught to soldiers and used in the field as needed. In the meantime, even though acceptance is slow and progress in treating PTSD conventionally even slower, EFT will forge ahead as a powerful treatment for those willing to move outside the "system" for their own sakes. As long as we're here, there will be help for anyone who seeks it.

Dr. Rossanna Massey's practice focuses exclusively now on the applications of EFT, especially the emotional underpinnings of serious diseases. She is available for private sessions, in-person or by phone (worldwide), lectures and workshops. Her website and additional information at EFTHelp.com.

Article Source: EzineArticles.com/expert/Dr. Rossanna M. Massey/623286
Article Source: EzineArticles.com/6810417

Unfortunately for service members, many military relationships and marriages fail due to the above reasons. Perhaps this is due to the horrible idea that spouses may not want to deal with the problems that service members face during deployments and when they return stateside. It is very safe to say that often times a service member returns home in a very different mental and sometimes physical state. It is not uncommon for the spouse to feel as if they can't deal with these kinds of issues, and thus they just don't feel like providing the support that the service member needs.

As citizens of this country, it is important that we stand behind our service members. Regardless of one's choice to support the war or not, it is important that we support our service members. Men and women voluntarily and happily dedicate themselves to lives of danger in order to protect the interests of the United States, knowing that relationships and marriages may fail, and that they are sacrificing a lot.

Expert Article:
Post-Traumatic Stress Disorder (PTSD) –
Let's Not Forget the Sufferer's Partner

When someone develops the mental health disorder known as PTSD after living through one or more traumatic events and he or she has a partner, that partner suffers right along with the other. In fact, while those who develop PTSD may experience depression, anxiety, difficulties related to role changes, communication problems, physical health issues, and turn to abusing substances to try and manage PTSD symptoms, did you know that the partner can develop these same problems?

However, if the partner is provided the knowledge and skills needed to become resilient, or to better adapt and cope with the challenges the unwanted guest of PTSD invariably brings into a relationship, these potential negatives could be avoided. Furthermore, the partner may discover that positives evolve from striving to effectively cope with the partner, the PTSD, and its impact on their relationship-such as a sense of mastery or self-efficacy.

Challenges the Partners of PTSD Sufferers Face

What challenges do partners of PTSD sufferers face? They typically fall into one or more of these categories:

- Coping with the changed personality and behaviors of the loved one with PTSD
- The lack of information and supportive services for partners of PTSD sufferers
- New financial strains and the likely burden of having to meet these alone
- The emotional or psychological strains associated with prolonged care-giving
- The social stigma of having a partner with a mental health disorder
- Challenges working with professionals providing services to the loved one with PTSD

Let's look at each category briefly, shall we?

Handling the Changed Personality and Behaviors of a Loved One with PTSD

PTSD changes the sufferer. That's not surprising when you consider that the disorder is defined by categories of symptoms that can have severe behavioral consequences. They are re-experiencing, avoidance, and hyperarousal.

What do we mean by re-experiencing? The PTSD sufferer is apt to have flashbacks of the traumatic event and/or to experience nightmares about it. Flashbacks, because they make the person believe he or she is in the midst of the traumatic event again, are something that PTSD sufferers want to avoid. Also, because PTSD sufferers do not know what will trigger their brains to engage in flashbacks, they often avoid activities or events they enjoyed previously-such as victims of sexual assault may want to avoid sex whereas war veterans may want to avoid crowds at malls and movie theatres.

Of course, the PTSD symptom of emotional numbing doesn't help matters, either. It results in PTSD sufferers not enjoying things they did previously. So, when you combine this with the desire to avoid situations that could potentially trigger flashbacks, doesn't it become more obvious why the PTSD sufferer may disappoint the partner and other family members by electing to stay home time and again versus going and doing things with them?

Another category of symptoms, hyperarousal, might be viewed as the PTSD sufferer's body essentially remaining in a fight or flight mode-or hypervigilant-long past the traumatic event. Because of hyperarousal, the PTSD sufferer may act irritated or angry much of the time. Needless to say, this can be quite upsetting to the partner who is trying to be loving and supportive.

Lack of Information and Supportive Services

Services have typically focused on the PTSD sufferer and tended to ignore the partner even though PTSD sufferers can benefit immensely from the support of a knowledgeable loved one. And of course, since both partners form a system that is adversely impacted when either partner is not functioning normally, partners should be seen as in need of help and services, too.

The resiliency of the partner of someone impacted by PTSD can be enhanced via education-about the mental disorder of PTSD, how it is treated, how to find the professionals who can provide the best treatments possible, as well as how to work with the helping professionals encountered. He or she can also then use this new knowledge to benefit the loved one with PTSD-as well as their relationship.

The partner of the PTSD sufferer not only has a lot of information to process, but the partner likely needs to develop some new skills. A self-help book I wrote, designated one of the "BEST BOOKS OF 2009" by the Library Journal, and entitled The Post-Traumatic Stress Disorder Relationship: How to Support Your Partner and Keep Your Relationship Healthy, provides the type of help partners need. It offers necessary information as well as teaches and models helpful skills. But then, part of the intent of this book is to help the partner to become more resilient in the face of challenges PTSD invariably brings into the relationship-a relationship which can suddenly seem as if it's with a stranger versus a loved one.

Coping with New Financial Strains

A PTSD sufferer may be incapable of attaining and maintaining the same type of job he or she did prior to developing this mental disability. Furthermore, many do not want to work around people as they did previously and instead, may seek to be outdoors working in nature, for instance. Certainly, such an environment may prove both calming and healing to the PTSD sufferer. That said, there also may not be jobs available that the PTSD sufferer can perform, they may pay less than the person made previously, or they may only be part-time. As a result, the burden of supporting the family may well fall on the partner's shoulders at a time when costs are likely increasing due to medical and other needs.

Where does the partner turn for help to learn how to cope with these new financial challenges? There is some information in The Post-Traumatic Stress Disorder Relationship that can help. However, government, state, and/or local agencies or not-for-profit organizations may be able to provide some necessary assistance-although many budgets are certainly being cut these days. Also, there's a government organization typically found in every county of this country that provides helpful information and guidance in this area-as well as others that should prove benefit couples impacted by PTSD. It's called Cooperative Extension. The partner can search for the nearest office by putting in the county's name, the state, and the words, Cooperative Extension. The local Extension Agent should be able to provide sound information that can help with budgeting, cost-cutting, and much more.

Combating the Emotional or Psychological Strains of Prolonged Care-Taking

For the PTSD sufferer to become more resilient in the face of his or her PTSD, it helps to pursue a lifestyle that is balanced or heals the body, mind, and spirit. This is certainly true for the partner as well. So, the PTSD-impacted couple may want to pursue some of these activities jointly-such as exercising regularly together. Or, for both of them to get in better touch with that part of the inner self that perpetuates healing and spiritual growth, they may want to spend time meditating or engaging in iRest Yoga Nidra together. iRest Yoga Nidra was developed by psychologist Richard C. Miller, Ph.D., and it has been used with enthusiasm and success by wounded warriors at Walter Reed. In fact, Dr. Miller told me when I called to ask him about this program, that many asked if their partners could participate in the classes with them.

The resilience of both individuals will also be enhanced by proper nutrition, adequate rest, and relaxation. Again, Cooperative Extension can provide information about preparing healthy meals-as can organizations such as the American Heart Association (AHA). In fact, AHA can also provide information about heart-healthy and stress-busting exercise. Needless to say, iRest Yoga Nidra will help with relaxation.

The Social Stigma of Having a Loved One with a Mental Disorder

Despite the efforts of advocates working on behalf of the mentally ill to overcome the stigma these individuals have faced in our society since its beginning, that stigma still exists.

Furthermore, as many a warrior with PTSD has discovered, while the military is striving to change the attitude that some have-that the development of PTSD signifies personal weakness or a character flaw-there is still much progress to be made. Therefore, while top military leaders may increasingly realize that PTSD is perhaps best viewed as akin to a chronic physical disease such as diabetes that requires ongoing management, not all those in supervisory positions accept that the person has become a victim of his or her brain. Unless the military can discover ways to build resilience so that people do not develop PTSD in the first place after experiencing ongoing trauma in the war zone, the best we can do is to help PTSD sufferers and their partners become resilient after the fact.

The partner needs to be prepared to deal with individuals who may cling to outdated beliefs as to why people develop PTSD. So, what is the partner going to say in response that will help educate versus cause the other person to become defensive-and remain steadfast in his or her current way of thinking? For guidance with this and other challenging tasks, the partner may want to contact the National Alliance on Mental Illness (NAMI). This organization continues to battle against social stigma for all people and families impacted by any mental illness.

Challenges Working with Medical and Mental Health Professionals

Professionals are often prepared to work with the PTSD sufferer, but less well equipped to work with the partner. Some professionals, rather than seeing the partner as someone who can support the PTSD sufferer and help him or her to jump on and walk that pathway toward recovery, may instead see the partner as someone who is apt to get in the way-or make the PTSD sufferer's recovery process more challenging yet. Of course, while this possibility certainly exists, the partner can also be educated so that as he or she becomes the professional's ally.

That said, if you are the partner struggling to work with a professional who sees you as the enemy, you may need to asset yourself. Let it be known that you intend to be actively involved in all matters associated with your loved one's care and recovery. Of course, there may be paperwork that your loved one needs to sign in order for professionals to talk to you about his or her medical issues.

It may also be necessary for you to attain a medical power of attorney. Why is this a good idea? Your loved one may be incapable of making sound medical decisions in his or her best interest. Let me provide a rather frightening example of why this could prove important-if not life-saving for your beloved.

There have been warriors wounded by PTSD given a cocktail of medications that so heavily sedated these individuals that they died in their sleep. I have communicated with one wife who took action to ensure this did not happen to her husband. Sadly enough, four warriors wounded by PTSD that her husband knew personally had died in this way-from ingesting a prescribed, yet lethal, cocktail of drugs. This concerned wife, however, because she had attained a medical power of attorney, saw to it that her husband's doctor removed him from these medications. But then, she had seen tell-tale signs that he was over-sedated. Needless to say, he was too sedated to take action in his own best interest.

How Helping Professionals Can Better Serve PTSD-impacted Couples

Are you a professional seeking to help couples impacted by PTSD? Well then, it's a good idea to measure family resiliency during your initial assessment by using resiliency, coping, and adaptation inventories. Once you have this information, you can help the couple to understand the type of challenges they're likely to face-to normalize these; then, begin to educate both parties regarding not only what they need to know about PTSD and its treatment, but teach and role-play skills that enhance sense of control and well-being-such as those found in The Post-Traumatic Stress Disorder Relationship. And certainly, teach them how to deal with other service providers. Talk about the goals they'd like to achieve as individuals and a couple-and then how to share these with professionals. What statements do they need to make, what questions should they ask?

Resiliency and the PTSD-impacted Couple

The partner of a PTSD sufferer who comes to learn healthy ways to cope with the PTSD and its impact on their relationship is apt to dismiss emotionally painful actions of the PTSD suffer as symptoms of the mental disorder versus taking them personally, will strive to do things that make it more comfortable for the PTSD sufferer to engage in activities, will help others to better accept the changed PTSD sufferer, and will elect not to dwell on the past or what the loved one was once capable of doing but instead, will come to accept that while life with a partner changed by PTSD is invariably different, their life together can nevertheless be meaningful and fulfilling.

Rather than fighting pain and change as many are inclined to do, the healthy partner of a PTSD sufferer will choose to believe that while there have been losses to endure, certainly, there have been – or likely will be – gains, too. Each negative event has a positive side or aspect, but one must look for it and seize it.

Both individuals in the PTSD-impacted couple may ultimately take pride in their ability to tackle and solve problems-or take pleasure in their newfound resiliency. And indeed, wouldn't that be a good positive to come out of this?

Dr. Diane England, author of "The Post-Traumatic Stress Disorder Relationship: How to Support Your Partner and Keep Your Relationship Healthy," designated one of the "BEST BOOKS OF 2009" by the "Library Journal," is a licensed clinical social worker. Dr. England will be speaking on how to help build resilience in PTSD-impacted couples at the Institute for Defense and Government Advancement's "Military Healthcare Convention and Conference" which will be held June 22-25, 2010 in San Antonio. She is pleased to be their media partner. For more information about this conference, Dr. England, or her book, go to www.PTSDRelationship.com.

Article Source: EzineArticles.com/expert/Dr._Diane_England/125769
Article Source: EzineArticles.com/3975041

Know that the support you provide as a military spouse is important. Being deployed is one of the most difficult parts of military service. You are away from your home, the people you love and in a place that may not welcome your presence. The job that you are doing is taxing, exhausting and draining, but is necessary to support the mission. With the help of support and therapy, preserving relationships and saving marriages is possible. So much has been lost in the service of this country so do everything you can to avoid adding your relationship to the list.

CHAPTER 5

Do I Stay or Do I Walk Away?

OVER THE COURSE OF A military career there are times where midcareer personnel have to make the choice of staying in the military or separating from service. This can be a difficult decision to make for a service member and it can be even more difficult when the service member is married and has children to consider.

Life as a military family means you are constantly moving. The moves you make over the course of a career impact not only you, but your family as well. Decisions have to be made such as if your spouse is going to work outside the home, or not work outside the home. A military spouse often needs more than just sitting at home waiting for their service member to come home. A military spouse needs a life of his or her own.

Sometimes that comes through working outside of the home. Sometimes that comes from raising a family. Sometimes it comes from volunteering and helping others. When you have found something that you enjoy and when you develop friendships, it can be hard to walk away from that and start all over again.

Being a military spouse means you have to do that over and over again. It can be frustrating and at a certain point sometimes you don't want to do it anymore. Introducing children into this environment makes the decision even tougher. Now you are not just making decisions for yourself. The decisions you are making impact those who depend upon you to choose for them. Children need to feel safe, they need consistency and it is up to you to ensure they are taken care of.

KHARYE J. POPE

Expert Article:
Mama, Mama Can't You See!
What the Military Has Done to Me!

Being a child of a parent serving in the military is difficult but being a dependent of two parents serving in the military is even more challenging. I can count on one hand the frugal times military children are recognized for serving alongside their parent(s) in the military. When we retire from our respective service is when our unit acknowledges out loud our children's sacrifices as well as to thank them for their service.

My personal story of life in the military is somewhat of a "whirlwind" of a story. Within a short time span I met my husband had our first child, got married, and then had a couple more children to add to the mix. In between all those intimate changes that consumed our personal life we also had to contend with moving to various duty assignment along the way.

Of course where ever we went our community was ready to thank us for our service and salute us for our dedication and sacrifice. Sure it was easy to recognize those who served as well as those still presently serving because we either wore our respective service memorabilia or don our uniforms. So we humbly thank our countrymen and women for recognizing us but I always wonder about our children.

How were they being recognized at school and throughout the community? Did their school understand how to integrate, educate, and matriculate our children in the educational system? Or are they subjected to the "catch all" transient care based on their school records? You know, their academic record that captures the many address changes in the system, the administrative reprimands (if any) to correct their disruption in class, and/or their social cognitive skills or lack thereof.

However, their school record doesn't tell the complete story. A story of losing a piece of their whole personality because each move affects their socialism. I remember candidly after the sixth daycare change and our oldest child was only three-years old and I saw the change in his personality.

Our oldest child came into this world literally with a smile on his face. Whenever he walked into a room, he always was the center of attention. From the time he was in my womb he knew how to dance and entertain a crowd. He learned how to walk at seven-months. Climb the stairs at nine-months and began to read at three-years old.

However, at the tender age of three, since he could think and speak for himself, he told me that he was scared. My child scared?! This can't be right, he always had a smile on his face and rolled with the punches every time we had to pack up and move. I didn't believe it yet I had to accept what he was stating and so I inquired further into the matter.

He was scared of not being liked and accepted by his classmates because he didn't know anyone and he was forever the new kid in the neighborhood and school. He didn't have the daycare stories to share with his classmates who for the most part went to the same daycare, played in the same leagues, or had any embarrassing stories to share with his classmates. He lacked the commonality shared amongst kids growing up in the same house/street who ran with the same crowd. I felt bad for him and guilty for serving at the same time. My husband and I told ourselves that he and now his siblings as well will be more resilient because of our military commitment, which is a true fact. Yet as a mother, I wanted to spare him the unnecessary personality change he would be subjected to all because of my military career; our military commitment.

From that moment, I vowed to always put my children's need first before my own, then serve and defend my countrymen and women, be the best wife I can be for my husband, and whatever time was left over in the day was reserved for me. As a parent serving in the military, we feel conflicted with our respective service values. Every being within tells us, country first, God second, and family last but how can that be? How can I focus on the mission at hand if I am consumed with the welfare of my family? These questions along with many more inundated my mind on a daily basis because I knew that my time in the military was quickly coming to an end.

KHARYE J. POPE

It is time for me to hang up my cover (hat), turn-in my uniform, and declined the next promotion.

Yet, I tussled with the unfairness of my career and the choices that I have to make; an all or nothing decree. As a leader, you are viewed by your peers as weak if you attempt to balance work life and family life; correction, as a female leader serving in the military you are at a disadvantage the moment you joined the Department of Defense (DoD). It is inevitable to silence a woman's decision to be a mother or even a man's choice in being a father. However, there is a huge disparity between the two genders.

More often than not, my male counterparts working within the Department of Defense/Department of Homeland Security whom are married have the luxury of having their wives handle the brunt of raising the children and taking care of home life. More often than none, the wives of my male counterparts are stay at home moms. Though they are consumed with stress of taking care of home life, then have the benefit of being there for their children unlike women serving in the military.

It is ironic that so much stride is made in allowing LGBT to serve openly in the military yet the same cannot be said of mothers or parents serving in the military. There needs to be more females with children or hands-on parent(s) appointed in Congress, in the Pentagon, and in every echelon of an organization. Simply promoting a "woman" doesn't cut the mustard.

I could share countless stories of female leaders who purposely declined to have kids because they had a dream of becoming the next "female general". Therefore, single women, men without children, or men who aren't active participants in their children's life cannot sympathize with the countless calendar juggling and career suicides that parent(s) in the military confront on a daily basis.

Overall, there needs to be an overhaul in how the military on a whole is structured and how we incorporate parent(s) in the formation. Long are the days where men were the breadwinner and women stayed home to take care of the home and raising the children. As early as 2000, DoD transitioned from a conducting one-mass deployment to implementing mini-size elements who possesses the same capabilities of a division size unit. I wish the same could be said for how we manage our diverse workplace. We spend millions if not trillions of dollars in to shaping DoD on a whole as an all-inclusive workforce yet we still allow leaders with archaic personal beliefs and values to run the business.

Article Source: EzineArticles.com/expert/Keisha_Teixeira/2106083
Article Source: EzineArticles.com/8979545

Decision Time

The older children get, the harder it can be to be constantly moving. It is hard always being the new kid in an environment. Not being able to have experienced what it means to have roots and being able to spend a number of years in one place not being able to spend 4 years in a high school. Not being able to form relationships in high school that will last a lifetime can impact teenagers greatly. It can be difficult feeling like an outsider and a significant factor that service members consider when making the decision to separate or to continue their careers.

Another factor that weighs heavily on service members with families contemplating leaving active service is the concerns of the military spouse. A significant burden and much sacrifice has been shouldered by the military spouse. Every time you have been deployed, they have also been deployed. Every time you have executed permanent change of station (PCS) orders, they have too. Every event of your military life has been experienced by your spouse. In many ways they have a great deal invested in your career. Their feelings matter.

Your military spouse may have put their aspirations and dreams on hold to support you in your career. At some point you are going to have to consider his or her needs. You may find yourself with an excellent opportunity outside of the military. You may love the military, but every service member has to realize that there will come a time when your military service ends. The question is when it does end what does your family look like?

CHAPTER 6

Managing Money

L IFE REQUIRES THAT WE MAKE choices. As a child, our choices are guided by our parents, as we get older we assume more responsibility for our choices. As an adult, the responsibility for our choices rests entirely on our shoulders. I had a First Sergeant that used to close all formations by saying "Think before you act because you will be held accountable for your actions." That has always stuck with me.

Everyone has their reasons for why they decided to join the military. Maybe you just wanted to leave the town you grew up in. Maybe you wanted money for college. Maybe you have a family tradition of military service. Whatever the reason you decided to join, the fact is it was your decision to raise your right hand and solemnly swear to affirm and defend the constitution of the United States of America. Now you have to do it.

The vast majority of enlisting personnel have not managed their finances for very long, and do not understand basic principles of managing money. This is the equivalent of handing a four-year old child who has played with toy guns their entire life a loaded handgun. I will clue you in on a secret… It is not going to end well.

How Childhood Experiences Influences Adult Behavior

To understand where you are going, you have to examine where you have been. Far too often we engage in crisis management rather than addressing the issues that are responsible for the crisis. It is not enough to look at your current situation and develop a plan for managing your current crisis. In order to implement a real and long lasting change, you have to do more than just manage the symptoms. What we often consider as dealing with the issue is mere triage. To really deal with the situation, we have to identify and address the root causes of the behavior that lead to our poor choices.

The roots of our attitudes towards money and finances are based on our upbringing. Our first financial role models are our parents/caregivers. We watch their behaviors and struggles which form the basis for how we handle money. The fact is that most parents don't discuss finances and managing money with their children. It's not that our parents/caregivers do not care. These discussions are not happening because the parents do not understand how to manage money themselves.

This is an important point. If you do not understand something and no one you know understands it either, then how can you teach someone else how to do it? The answer is you can't. You cannot fault someone for exhibiting bad behavior if they have never been taught otherwise. That being said with the wealth of knowledge available, there is no excuse for not educating yourself with a basic working knowledge at the very least. There are few things as personal and as important as the relationship we maintain with our own finances. Taking a little time now can save you a lot of money later. Reading this book is a good first step.

Saving money is like going to the gym. If you are serious about physical fitness as a means to lose weight, get into better shape, improve self-esteem, etc. you will establish a workout routine. You figure out how many days a week you are going to work out and which muscle groups you plan to focus on; and how long your workout will last.

You change your eating habits. You eliminate certain foods and reduce the amount of food you eat at meals. Eat smaller portion; and drink more water. The most critical element of your diet and physical fitness routine is the discipline required to maintain it. You are putting in work today to obtain results in the future. You deal with the sweat, soreness and fatigue because you know that the result that you are seeking is worth the sacrifice.

Saving money requires the same discipline. Instead of seeing the results as a physically fit and stronger body, the result of saving money impacts so many aspects of your life. The fact is that we all have a limited amount of resources (i.e. time, money, food, etc.). What separates the successful from those who fail is how we allocate/deploy those resources. When you make the decision to save money, you are committing to setting aside some amount for the future rather than spending that money today. So why would someone consider doing this when there is so much cool stuff you can buy right now?

As hard as it may be to imagine, there are times when the unexpected happens. We live in an age where credit cards and long-term financing make obtaining the things that we want easier. The truth is we have a greater appreciation for what we struggle for because we had to work for it. The more sweat equity you have invested into your aspiration results in greater satisfaction when the goal is achieved.

There is a catch associated with overreliance on credit cards and long-term financing. The catch is that by the time you pay for the purchase (principle and interest) the amount you have paid greatly exceeds the original purchase price (Insert a specific example of financing). Obviously it is best to pay cash, but that requires the patience to save the money.

We live in a world of advertising and marketing that tells you that you can have everything you want right now. We live in a microwave world of instant gratification. No pain and suffering is needed to lose weight. Just have that surgical procedure done. No need to save for a car, you can get 100% dealer financing with the dealer's preferred lender. Everybody has a mortgage, credit cards, car loans or other financing payments. We have stopped looking at the full price of what we are buying. We are only concerned with what the weekly/monthly payment will be.

That is extremely shortsighted and quite expensive. The amount of interest you are paying is keeping you from being able to afford what you need in the present and more importantly the future. You are still paying for what you bought in the past instead of enjoying the present and more importantly the future. The amount of debt you carry relative to your income has a severe impact on the range of choices you have today and in the future.

Having too much debt impacts and increases the difficulty when trying to rent an apartment, obtain a mortgage, and determine insurance rates. Having too much debt may result in a higher interest rate on a loan, keep you from getting a job or a promotion, or make you ineligible to obtain a security clearance, or pass a background check. It isn't that debt is always a terrible thing. Demonstrating the ability to responsibly manage a number of different types of credit accounts is a critical skill that will make a range of opportunities available to you.

It is a lot easier to get a loan from a bank if you don't need a loan from a bank. I know that it sounds crazy, but it is the truth. Banks like to lend when they are certain they will get their money back. If you are financially healthy then you are much more likely to have a loan or credit application approved. So what exactly does being financially healthy look like?

Businesses and Financial Institutions have developed a scoring model that is used to predict or determine credit worthiness. This scoring model is commonly referred to as FICO scoring. FICO scores are based on consumer credit files of the three major credit bureaus (Equifax, Experian and TransUnion).

There is no such thing a single FICO score as each credit bureau uses the information they have in their files on you. There are, at the time of this writing, 42 different credit scores for a consumer. Although the exact formula used to calculate your FICO score is secret, we know that 35% of your score is based on payment history; 30% of your score is based on debt burden; 15% of your score based on the length of your credit history; 10% of your score is based on the types of credit used; and 10% is based on recent inquires (i.e. hard searches of credit).

A higher credit limit is better for your score because it can lower the rate of credit utilization. Credit utilization is the percentage of credit that you are currently utilizing. Overall credit utilization is the total amount owed on all your credit cards divided by the total limit of all of your credit cards. Individual credit card utilization is the amount owed on a particular credit card divided by the limit on the credit card. Say you have a credit card with a $15,000 limit. You currently owe $3250. Your credit utilization rate for the card is 21.67%. The FICO score model awards higher scores to individuals with credit utilization rates lower than 30%.

The Generic or "Classic" FICO score model ranges from 300-850 and the higher the score the lower the risk associated with doing business with the score holder. As a result of the Fair and Accurate Transactions (FACT) Act you are entitled to obtain a copy of your credit report from each of the three credit bureaus once a year by visiting annualcreditreport.com. You then have an opportunity to ensure that the information contained within is accurate. If you find any information that is not correct you have the right to dispute the information you think is wrong. Your credit score is not included in your credit report, but you have an opportunity to purchase your score from each of the 3 credit bureaus.

What Information is Included in Your Credit Report?

Personal Information
Compiled from credit applications you've filled out, this information normally includes your name, current and recent addresses, Social Security Number, date of birth, and current and previous employers.

Credit History
The bulk of your credit report consists of details about credit accounts that were opened in your name or that list you as an authorized user (such as a spouse's credit card). Account details, which are supplied by creditors with

which you have an account, include the date the account was opened, the credit limit or amount of the loan, the payment terms, the balance, and a history that shows whether or not you've paid the account on time. Closed or inactive accounts, depending on the manner in which they were paid, stay on your report for 7 to 11 years from the date of their last activity.

Credit Report Inquiries

Credit reporting agencies record an inquiry whenever your credit report is shown to another party, such as a lender, service provider, landlord, or insurer. Inquiries remain on your credit report for up to two years.

Public Records

Matters of public record obtained from government sources such as courts of law including liens, bankruptcies, and overdue child support may appear on your credit report. Most public record information stays on your credit report for 7 years.

What is Not Included in Your Credit Report?

A credit report does not include information about your checking or savings accounts, bankruptcies that are more than 10 years old, charged-off or debts placed for collection that are more than seven years old, gender, ethnicity, religion, political affiliation, medical history, or criminal records. Your credit score is generated by information on your credit report, but is not part of the report itself.

Who Can Look at Your Credit Report?

Anyone with what is considered a permissible purpose can look at your report. These companies, groups, and individuals include:

- Potential lenders
- Landlords
- Insurance companies

- Employers and potential employers (usually only with your written consent)
- Companies you allow to monitor your credit report for signs of identity theft
- Some groups considering your application for a government license or benefit
- A state or local child support enforcement agency
- Any government agency (may be allowed to view only certain portions)
- Someone using your credit report to provide a requested product or service
- Someone that has your written authorization to obtain your credit report

Correcting Errors in Your Credit Report

It's possible for incorrect, incomplete or outdated information to appear on your credit report. If it does, it can drastically lower your chances of getting the loans, credit cards, and other credit products you deserve. If you find an error, take the following steps as soon as possible. If you see evidence of fraud, contact the credit reporting companies immediately. Explain the situation and ask that a fraud alert be placed in your file. Also report the fraud to the police, and your creditors.

1. Contact the Credit Reporting Company

Contact the credit reporting company that is reporting the item in question. It is helpful for you to have a printed copy of your credit report from them. You may be eligible to receive it free of charge.

After you advise the credit reporting agency of the information that you are disputing and why, the credit reporting company will review it. If you have any documentation that supports your position also send that to the credit reporting agency. If further investigation is required, the credit reporting agency will provide notification of what you're disputing to the source that furnished the disputed information to them.

The source of the disputed information will review the information, conduct its own investigation, and report back to the credit reporting agency. The credit reporting company will then make all appropriate changes to your credit file based on the investigation, and notify you of the results of the investigation and any changes that were made to your credit report.

2. Contact the Creditor Regarding the Problem

In some cases, you should contact the appropriate creditor or lender before contacting a credit reporting company. This is especially true if you are a victim of identity theft or fraud. You should also contact the appropriate creditor or lender if that source has verified the information that you disputed with the credit reporting company. Most large creditors have standard procedures for customers to dispute items about their accounts with them. If you have proof that the item in question is incorrect, it should be resolved quickly.

If the creditor finds that the disputed information is indeed incorrect, the creditor is required by federal law, the Fair Credit Reporting Act, to update its records both internally and with the credit reporting companies to which it reported the disputed information, usually within 30 days.

Always follow up your phone calls with a letter. List each disputed item, and state how it is inaccurate, attaching copies of all relevant documents. Include your full name, account number, the dollar amount in question, and the reason you believe the item is wrong. Be concise.

3. Contact the Other Credit Reporting Companies

If you find an inaccuracy with one credit reporting company, you may want to get your credit report from the other two credit reporting companies to see if their credit reports contain the same error. After you've corrected an error with one credit reporting company, the other credit reporting companies will in most cases, also receive the corrected information. But for prompt correction, it's best to contact each of the three major credit reporting companies yourself.

4. Make Sure the Disputed Information is Addressed

Within 30 days (45 days if based upon your annual free credit file), the credit reporting company should notify you of the results of its investigation. You'll need to obtain a new copy of your credit report to make sure the inaccuracies have been corrected or removed. If the disputed information has been resolved, you can have the credit reporting company notify anyone who received a credit report with inaccurate information in the past six months (two years in the case of employers) of the corrections that have been made.

5. If You Cannot Resolve a Disputed Item

You have the right to file a brief statement with the consumer reporting company, free of charge, explaining the nature of your disagreement. The consumer reporting company may limit your statement to not more than 100 words if it provides you with assistance in writing a clear summary of the disagreement. Your statement will become part of your credit report, and will be reported each time your credit report is accessed, for as long as the disputed item remains in your credit report.

How Poor Decisions Can Negatively Impact Your Finances

We have all been guilty of making poor decisions and those decisions often have a negative impact on your finances and credit. A lot of people were overextended and lost a great deal of net worth during the recession/housing crisis that started in 2008. People lost their homes and in some cases, lost a significant portion of the life savings/retirement. Individuals took on more than they were able to handle based on the belief that the value of their homes would continue to increase.

The fact is the law of gravity always applies and that everything that goes up eventually comes down. We were all sold on the idea of everyone having their own piece of the American Dream. We were assured that home ownership was the first step to becoming an entrenched part of the middle class. We were told to buy the most house you can afford, even though we may not have needed a house of that size. We lost the ability to distinguish a need from a want and that hubris contributed to so many people losing so much.

The ability to distinguish between something that we need as opposed to what it is that we desire is an essential part of making good financial decisions. We need to eat, we need housing and we need clothing. We want an expensive five course meal, we want a 5,000 square foot house, and we want a custom made closet full of designer clothes and shoes. While our finances may support our needs they rarely allow us to obtain all of our wants. As a result, we have to prioritize and budget to balance our needs and wants with respect to our finances.

We see our friends and neighbors with the things that we want and feel that we are not as successful as they are because we lack these things. In order to feel better about ourselves, in order to elevate ourselves in the eyes and opinions of others we find a way to obtain some of the things we see the people around us having. Since we lack the money to purchase these items outright, we result to alternative financing means.

The first tool in the living beyond our means toolkit is credit cards. We max out the credit cards we have. We apply for an increased credit limit on the cards we have. We apply for new credit cards. We initiate balance transfers to different cards. We draw cash advances from credit cards.

A second tool in the living beyond our means toolkit is a home equity line. The difference between what a home is currently worth and the amount that is owed on the house is the amount of equity that has been accumulated in the home. A home equity line is a line of credit that is some percentage of the home's equity. As long as the home equity line is not borrowed against, you do not have to make any payments.

A third tool in the living beyond our means toolkit is a home equity loan. A home equity loan is a fixed amount of money borrowed which is based on the amount of equity you have in the home. Payments are fixed and constant for the duration of loan beginning when the loan is issued.

A fourth tool in the living beyond our means toolkit is mortgage financing/refinancing. There are many kinds of mortgage financing/ refinancing options such as fixed rate loans, adjustable rate loans, interest-only loans, cash-out refinancing, reverse mortgages, and second mortgages. There are situations where the use of these products does make sense, but far too many people have been and are still being steered to products that are not appropriate for their financial situation.

There are cases where people have fallen for exotic financial products (i.e. sub-prime loans) even though they are eligible for fundamentally sound financial products with more favorable rates (i.e. prime loans). This has happened and continues to happen because individuals placed their trust into people who were more concerned with enriching themselves than helping the people who came to them seeking financial advice and/or assistance.

Another tool in the living beyond our means toolkit designed for individuals of limited means is what is I consider financing of the last resort – predatory lending. Examples of predatory lending products provided by the lenders of last resort include but are not restricted to payday loans, pawn shops, and title loans. Individuals who get caught up in this kind of lending are the ones who can afford it the least.

A large segment of the population is barely hanging on to a middle class existence. Far too many of us are living paycheck to paycheck and are not certain how all of our bills are going to be paid. Finances are so tight that a visit to the hospital can push a family that is just barely holding on into a dangerous situation. Unfortunately, when things go wrong it is never just one thing at a time. When bad things happen, a series of unfortunate events normally occur over a short period of time.

Imagine a single parent working as wait staff has a sick child. The single parent has to take the child to the emergency room due to a lack of insurance. The single parent has no sick leave or vacation time and works at a job that does not have family friendly work policies. The single parent explains the situation, but is told don't worry about coming back to work because they no longer have a job.

Now the single parent has a sick child, a hospital bill and no job. Shortly thereafter the single parent's car breaks down. The car needs a new starter, but the single parent cannot afford it. The single parent's credit has a number of missed and late payments due to a failed marriage which left the single parent with poor credit. The single parent has few options available.

It is not that the hypothetical single parent is a bad person. A combination of bad luck and poor decisions regarding relationships and finances led the single parent to the situation we discussed above. This is just an illustration of how easy it can be to find yourself in a situation where you have very limited options and are forced to turn to a predatory financing option. Once you find yourself in a situation like this it is not easy to pull yourself out of this destructive cycle. The best solution is to make decisions that prevent you from ever getting in this situation to begin with.

Far too often we allow life to happen to us instead of dictating how we move forward in life. We always react instead of imposing a proactive stance. By assuming a reactive posture, we are accepting whatever happens as being inevitable. The fact is that nothing is further than the truth. We all have the capacity within ourselves to mold and shape our existence. The size and scope of our accomplishments is constrained only by our vision and the determination we have to make it into our reality.

So what drives us to spend money we don't have on things we don't need and cannot afford. We seek validation of ourselves in the eyes and opinions of those who matter to us. We want to be considered successful, prosperous and respected. This is often done though the display of material items. The mindset is that if you have the items associated with wealth then you must be wealthy. It doesn't matter if you don't have two nickels to rub together. The only thing that matters is the illusion you present.

The mindless pursuit of the illusion over that which is substantive has lead to the financial ruin of countless individuals. We tend to use material items to substitute for the shortfalls and voids in our personal and professional lives. Sometimes we spend in an attempt to make up for neglecting those who are important to us. Sometimes we spend because we are trying to make someone happy. Sometimes we spend because we are trying to solve the problems of other people even though we have our own problems. Sometimes we spend because we feel guilty that we are more fortunate than those we care for.

The reason why we allow ourselves to become over extended is not nearly as important as the reason why we continue to remain that way. The only person that can answer that question is you. Fortunately, you have the chance to answer the question if you have the courage to confront the problem.

Making the decision to focus on your own financial health is not being selfish. The decision to focus on your own financial help is the first step in selfing. You cannot help someone else if you need help yourself. You have an obligation to provide for yourself so you are not a burden on those who love you. Once that obligation is met, if you have the means and the desire to do so, then you can consider if you are willing to help someone else.

People love strong people because strong people never ask for anything. Regardless of whatever difficulty they have they find a way to deal with it. Strong people are the rocks that others gravitate towards. They provide stability in a sea of chaos. They pick people up and carry them when they cannot continue on alone. However, sometimes you can help too much which prevents the person you care about from developing the ability to solve their own problems. A classic example of this is being a co-signer for a relative who always seems to be in financial difficulty.

They default and you are left paying back the loan. Once that occurs you are left to pick up the pieces and try to move on.

Reestablishing Your Creditworthiness

Bad credit can happen to good people. Don't despair if it has happened to you. There are ways you can get your creditworthiness in shape over time. But you have to start working on it today—and keep working hard to show potential lenders that you're serious about getting your ability to take on credit in order. As you do so, your creditworthiness should improve and that could result in better credit offers and a savings in money. There are no quick fixes to improve your creditworthiness because accurate and timely credit information generally cannot be removed from your credit report. By improving creditworthy behavior going forward and over time, you may be able reestablish your creditworthiness and credit capacity. There are a number of things that you can do that may help. Here is how to get started:

Open New Accounts and Pay Them Off

Being able to repay a variety of new accounts is a key step in rebuilding your creditworthiness. That means devising a strategy to open and pay off as many different kinds of accounts as you can is better than adding more debt to an existing credit card.

Start Small

Reestablishing your creditworthiness can be similar to starting over from scratch, and starting small may be the easiest option. Credit cards from department stores or your local credit union can be useful.

Consider Asking for Help

If you can't qualify for credit on your own, ask a friend or family member to cosign for a small loan or credit card. If you can stay current on a major credit card account or small auto loan, this will speed up the process of re-establishing good credit on your own.

Consider a Secured Credit Card

They are guaranteed by a deposit that you make with the credit grantor. Secured cards offer the purchasing power of a major credit card. Just make sure the grantor reports payment histories to the three major credit reporting bureaus so you're building your positive payment history.

Use Your New Accounts in Moderation

And make payments that are more than the minimum. You can keep a small balance so that your positive payment history will continue to show up on your credit report.

Keep Your Balances Low

Avoid carrying a balance that is more than 30% of your credit limit (lenders may view it as excessive debt that you may not be able to stay current with).

Reduce Your Household Spending

Review your household expenses and determine which ones you could do without. Consider creating a budget to track exactly where your money goes each month.

Call Lenders if You Can't Pay Some of Your Debts

Explain your situation and many of the lenders may be willing to work out a plan for you to pay back what you owe.

Contact a Credit Counselor to Make a Plan For Paying Off Credit Bills

Beware of agencies that offer "quick fix" ways to get out of debt.

Be Patient – The Payoff is Worth it

It takes some time for your new creditworthiness to gain momentum. You are demonstrating that you are not depending on certain credit cards and loans for your financial survival. That's why opening and paying down accounts may make it a little easier to get more credit. With patience and timely repayments, you'll likely be able to reestablish your creditworthiness so that lenders will look favorably when making decisions about your ability to handle even more credit.

What we are talking about is making a lifestyle change. You have accumulated a lifetime of bad financial habits with the debt and the issues that come with those habits. It is foolish to believe that you can continue to engage in the same kinds of behavior and "fix your credit". Even if you were to win the lottery (which is highly unlikely) you would soon find yourself in the same position you were in before you won the lottery because you are still engaging the same financial habits you were using before you won the lottery.

Despite what you may be told, you cannot take control of your finances without experiencing the pain resulting from dealing with the mess you created. It's not pretty, it is not sexy, and it is hard. It is supposed to be. Sometimes we learn more from our mistakes than our successes. Having overcome difficult circumstances through our own efforts we are reluctant to make the same mistakes again. The lessons learned through struggle are never truly forgotten.

Taking Control of Your Finances

Everyone has had a time where there are more bills than there is money to pay them. It seems that no matter what you do there is never enough money to pay everything. When you are struggling to keep the lights on, the idea of saving for retirement and saving money for your children's education seems like a pipe dream. As soon as the money comes in, you find it being spent leaving you wondering what you are working for.

I'd love to be able to share with you some magical secrets to turn your situation around, but I cannot. If I had to draw a parallel it would be some weight loss guru telling you that you can lose weight by taking a magic pill without changing your lifestyle or eating habits. It just isn't so. You are going to have to do some soul searching and examine exactly where you are spending money.

The first thing you need to do is identify what you actually need in order to survive. Maslow's hierarchy of needs indicates that on a biological and physiological level, basic life needs are air, food, drink, shelter, warmth, sex and sleep. You need to spend money to eat, drink, on housing and to keep warm or cool. What you have control over is how much you spend on these needs.

All of this brings us to the dreaded B-word... Budget. It is one of the most irritating and depressing things to do, but it is a vital step if you are serious about taking control of your finances. So how do you go about making your budget?

All successful budgets require understanding where your money is going so you need to figure out how you spend your money. Tracking how you spend your money over a month gives you a good frame of reference of how you spend your money. It requires discipline to track everything you spend money on for a month. Saving receipts or billing statements to track how much and how often you spend provides a model of your behavior.

Once you have evidence reflecting your spending habits then you can sit down and figure out your recurring monthly bills and identify your income sources. Let's assume that you are an E-5 with no dependents with more than 6 years of service and are stationed in the Washington D.C. area.

E-5 with no dependents	
Base Pay	$2,761.88
Basic Assistance for Housing (BAH)	$2,286.00
Basic Assistance for Sustenance (BAS)	$367.92
Total	$5,415.80

Keep in mind that the total shown is before any taxes have been taken out. BAH and BAS are considered to be non-taxable income. Assuming that you are in the 28% tax bracket your take home base pay is actually $1,988.55. The total of your base pay, BAH and BAS is $4,642.47. Having determined how much you earn from military pay and allowances we can now look at taking the information you gathered on you spending habits and see where your money is going.

We are going to break down expenses into four separate categories:

- Loans and/or Debt
- Insurance Premiums
- Utilities
- Miscellaneous

Expenses that we are including under Loans and/or Debt are:

- Mortgage or Rent
- Credit Cards
- Home Equity Loan/Home Equity Line
- Car Loan
- Student Loans

Expenses that we are including under Insurance Premiums are:

- Life
- Auto
- Home
- Health (including Disability)
- Long Term Care

Expenses that we are including under Utilities are:

- Electricity
- Gas

- Telephone
- Cable
- Internet
- Water & Sewer

Expenses that we are including under Miscellaneous are:

- Groceries
- Child Care
- Vacation
- Entertainment
- Clothing
- Gas
- Commuting
- Charity
- Pocket Money

Using the information you gathered on your spending and expenses and the information we have obtained about your income sources, we can generate a budget. Having identified how much you owe (total and monthly) and after establishing how you make those payments from your income sources, you can then see what you have left over. From this amount you establish categories of what is important to you (e.g. entertainment, savings and retirement).

As difficult as it may be, you need to establish a habit of automatic savings. This is what is known as paying yourself first. Exactly how much you pay yourself depends on your situation, but a good place to start is 10% of your base pay. It is generally best that you establish an automatic draft to an account that you do not have easy access to. This reduces the temptation to spend this money on something frivolous. Establishing an emergency fund provides you with a cushion that you can use when you need it.

After establishing an emergency fund, you can take a look at what you have left and decide what your goals are. Having identified what your goals are, you can start setting money aside to fund those goals. Once all of your goals have been funded whatever is left over you can consider as discretionary funds. Unfortunately, the mere act of creating a budget is not going to solve your problems. You must have the conviction and discipline to stick to it. A budget is only a tool, it cannot fix your problems. The only way that happens is if you make it happen.

Financial Irresponsibility and How it Impacts You

You may not be aware of all of the ways that financial irresponsible behavior can impact your day to day life. Having poor credit can limit the choices available to you personally and professionally. If you are trying to get a new apartment, the first thing the apartment manager does is check your credit. If your credit score is below what the apartment manager deems as an acceptable level, you are not getting the apartment.

If you are trying to get a new car if your credit score is considered sub-prime, you will have to pay a much higher rate of interest to get a loan. If you are trying to open a bank account and your credit score is too low, you may find you are unable to open a bank account and develop a relationship with a bank. If you are considering buying a house, you will not be able to qualify for a loan.

Financial irresponsibly also has consequences in your professional life. You may find yourself not being able to obtain a security clearance as your financial irresponsibility makes you susceptible to being blackmailed or unable to hold a position of public trust. You may also find yourself passed over for promotions because if you cannot display the responsibility to deal with your finances, how can you be entrusted to be a leader.

Identifying a Financial Mentor to Learn From

A key part of learning about money is identifying a role model – a financial mentor who you can emulate and pattern your behavior on. You can do this passively by learning about someone in the public domain via books, magazines or some other form of media; or you can be more proactive by personally identifying someone and initiating contact. The second approach while requiring more work in all likelihood, will lead to a much more rewarding relationship. A simple definition of a financial mentor is someone who manages money effectively, and is willing to talk to you about how the person deals with their finances.

I am going to share something with you. People tend to enjoy talking about what they do well. If you approach the individual that you have targeted with interest and sincerity they may take the time to answer your questions assuming they have the time. This requires that you have taken the time to figure out what questions to ask.

Everyone has a different level of financial literacy and draws from their individual pool of financial knowledge. The depth of that pool is determined by your upbringing and background. If you don't have a deep pool to draw from you can always add water to your pool. There is no reason to be embarrassed by what you do not know. No one knows everything about everything. The only reason you should be embarrassed is if you choose not to add to your pool after realizing the importance of it. Considering the sheer volume of financial information available from reputable and knowledgeable sources there is no excuse for failing to do so.

Even if you are concerned about personal embarrassment, consider the other people who can benefit from your stepping outside of your comfort zone. Potential beneficiaries include your spouse or significant other, any children that you have (or will have in the future), your parents and/or extended family. You are doing this for reasons that are bigger than you. The financial habits that you practice are observed by everyone you come into contact with. You have a larger influence on the people you care about than you may realize.

So what are the questions you should ask? You may not like this, but the answer is that it depends. Keep in mind that in order to ask an intelligent question you have to know what you do not know. That means you have to do research. You have to read and seek information so you can formulate the questions to get the answers you want.

Understanding the fundamentals of banking (i.e. What is the difference between a debit card and a credit card?), investing (i.e. what is the difference between a stock and a bond), and mortgages (i.e. what is the difference between an ARM and a FHA loan?) allows a potential financial mentor to take your questions seriously. Once you are taken seriously you are more likely to get the results you are seeking.

Credit and Your Spouse

It is not a coincidence that over half of marriages end in divorce. The leading cause of divorce is infidelity. Infidelity has many faces, but the toll that financial infidelity can be just as if not more destructive than the sense of betrayal caused by learning your spouse has been cheating on you. Financial infidelity can be committed by men and women although the reasons that each engage in it differ. The sad truth is that we spend more time watching football (men); and shopping for wardrobe items (women) than we spend listening and more importantly, hearing what each other has to say.

People search for fulfillment outside of their marriage because there is something that is missing within the marriage. At the beginning of the relationship, there was something that brought you and your spouse together. The longer you are together the more likely you are to begin to take one another for granted and you stop doing the things that let each other know how much they mean to you.

As time progresses, you lose sight of the reason you were drawn to each other in the first place. You stop being partners working together to achieve a common goal and essentially become roommates. The partnership that formed the foundation of your relationship is cracking and ignoring the problem is not going to solve it.

The key to having a healthy marriage is effective communication. You have to be secure enough in your relationship to engage in honest communication especially when it comes to money. When you or your spouse is feeling ignored or insecure in the marriage they may engage in behavior that is destructive to the marriage and your finances.

Feeling unfulfilled, your spouse may spend money that you are unaware of. It is possible that they may make purchases and hide them from you, open credit cards and/or bank accounts that serve as their "rainy day" fund and/or exit strategy in anticipation of the marriage falling apart. They may lie and tell you that bills are being paid, but divert that money for their own purposes.

Spending can be just as addictive as alcohol, food or drugs. The rush someone feels, the endorphins that are released are just as potent as what is felt when someone consumes alcohol, food or drugs. For that brief moment, the void that exists in the marriage is filled with the excitement, the rush that comes from a new purchase. The problem is that the rush, the "high" does not last.

In order to recapture that "high", you have to make another purchase, and then another. The problem is that every time you buy something, the "high" associated with that purchase doesn't last as long. In order to make up for the fading "high", the value of the purchase has to increase or the volume of purchases has to increase. Regardless of what you do, it is an empty solution to the real problem, the issue in your marriage. Until the core issue is identified, addressed and resolved, the destructive pattern of behavior will continue. You will continue to be unhappy and make your significant other miserable as well.

Two distinct and separate individuals transitioning and forming a partnership is difficult. Losing the ability to do what you want when you want to do it and having to take into consideration what someone else thinks and/or needs is not easy. Unfortunately, that is what is necessary to do if you are going to have trust regarding financial matters. Both parties must be involved in managing household finances.

Serious discussions must be held related to financial expectations, and a written contract outlining what was agreed upon can be helpful as a point of reference. Knowing where the money is and how much is there is important so that if something were to happen to either of you, the other would know how to manage household affairs.

Your marriage changes once you have children. It is no longer all about the two of you. You now have to put the needs of others ahead of your own. Your financial priorities have changed, and your behavior needs to reflect that. If you were having difficulty with financial infidelity and open communication before, adding children to the mix takes it to a whole new level.

Prior to the 1990-1991 Persian Gulf War, General Colin Powell expressed a series of questions that came to be known as the "Powell Doctrine". The doctrine is a series of questions that all have to be answered affirmatively before taking military action and are as follows:

1. Is a vital national security interest threatened?
2. Do we have a clear attainable objective?
3. Have the risks been fully and frankly analyzed?
4. Have all the other non-violent policy means been fully exhausted?
5. Is there a plausible exit strategy to avoid endless entanglement?
6. Have the consequences of our actions been fully considered?
7. Is the action supported by the American people?
8. Do we have broad international support?

All of these questions have to be answered yes in order to authorize military action. While the handling of your family's personal finances does not equate to weighing the costs associated with waging war, the concepts expressed in the Powell Doctrine can be reworked to address your own financial situation:

1) Is this purchase something that is a need or is it a want?
There is a difference between something that we need versus something that we want. Due to advertisers, marketing and popular culture too many of us have lost the ability to differentiate between the two.

2) How does this purchase further my financial goals?
Take the time to examine the rationale for why you are making the purchase. Being honest about how what you are buying impacts your budget, your finances, and your marriage will save you from a great deal of heartache later. If you come to the conclusion that the purchase does not further your goals an honest assessment of if it is something we can actually afford or even need should be undertaken.

3) What is the opportunity cost associated with this purchase?
The question you should be asking is simple. If this purchase is made, what necessary item or goal will we not be moving toward? If the answer is something of significance then you may want to reconsider the purchase.

4) Is there a way that I can obtain this without having to buy it (i.e. barter or trade)?
If you have the ability to obtain something without having to pay cash for it, this is always preferable. Utilizing the skills you have to obtain the things you need or want allows you to save your money for when you need it most.

5) Is this a depreciable asset or something that retains or increases in value?
If you are buying something that depreciates substantially the moment you take possession (i.e. a brand new sports car), you might want to consider if there an alternative that has already depreciated that is just as effective as the greatly depreciated asset (e.g. the same sports car that is 3 years old).

6) How is this purchase going to impact my finances and my ability to meet my preexisting financial commitments?
You have given your word or may have signed a contract that obligates you to repay an outstanding debt in accordance with an established schedule. If what you are purchasing impacts your ability to meet your

preexisting commitments (i.e. child support), then you may run into issues with the court system and your command.

7) Does my immediate family agree with or support the purchase?
Your financial choices impact the people you love. As your choices impact them, they do have an interest in what you purchase and how you manage your finances. Their input must be weighed in any major financial decision.

8) Does my extended family agree with or support the purchase?
See the reasons described in number 7 above.

The term opportunity cost is an economic concept. It assumes that an individual who is faced with a number a choices selects what the individual considers to be the best choice. All the other choices are compared to the selected choice and a difference in value between the choices is determined.

As an example, a recent college graduate is faced with a choice between going to graduate school or using the newly obtained college degree to obtain work. The graduate decides to go to graduate school. A possible opportunity cost in this case would be the salary the student would have earned by working for the period the student is enrolled in school. There are many opportunity costs associated with marriage.

Marriage and Credit

Managing your credit can be tricky, even when you're the only person involved in your financial decisions. When you add a spouse to the mix, you have to be extra careful to ensure that your credit remains in good standing.

Discuss Your Financial Status

First of all, both you and your spouse should put all your financial records – savings, salaries, investments, real estate and especially credit – on the table. If one of you has a less-than-glowing credit history, it will affect the other as soon as you start applying for credit together and opening joint accounts. Reviewing your credit reports together help prevent any unpleasant surprises in the future. In addition, your new joint accounts will appear on both of your credit reports in the future, so be sure to pay careful attention to your bills and pay them on time.

To Merge or not to Merge Accounts

Once you've aired your credit laundry, you'll need to decide whether or not to merge all your financial accounts. Many couples do this because consolidated accounts are easier for record-keeping. Points to keep in mind include the following:

Both of you are responsible for all debt incurred in any joint credit accounts. Regardless of who's incurring debt, a missed payment on a joint account will negatively affect both of your records. The same is true in community property states, where virtually any debt entered into during marriage is automatically considered joint.

If you miss a payment on an individual account, that payment may impact your ability to open joint accounts because both credit histories will be considered. If you decide to consolidate your accounts, you might want to keep at least one credit account in your own name as a safeguard in the event of an emergency. Keeping an individual account can also be a good thing in the event of divorce to re-establish an individual credit history.

Benefits of Having Individual Accounts When Married

The key to successful credit management as a couple is understanding that your individual credit behavior affects both you and your partner. To ensure that you are able to quickly get credit at the best possible terms, be sure you both understand all the implications that accompany a joint account. In addition, consider how the payments stemming from a major credit purchase will affect your overall budget.

Women who take their husband's surname after getting married need to notify the Social Security Administration and their current creditors of this change. You do not need to notify the credit reporting agencies of a name change. They will automatically will update the name on a credit report when creditors report it.

CHAPTER 7

Financing Major Purchases

Buying a Home – Plan in Advance

Buying a home is likely to be the largest purchase you will ever make. It can be complicated and stressful, but with careful planning, buying a home can be a more satisfying process. To help you plan for this major purchase, this is a list of essential steps to take toward achieving your dream of homeownership.

Get Your Credit Report

Before approving your request for a home loan, mortgage lenders review your credit report. In fact, they often get your report from two or more credit reporting companies to be sure they have your complete credit history. It is a good idea to review your credit report in advance to see your credit from a lender's perspective. That can help you avoid possible loan approval delays. If you are thinking of buying a home, it's a good idea to check your credit report in the months before you apply for home loan financing. Are there inaccuracies on your credit report? File a dispute and clear your report.

Be Prepared to Answer Questions

Here is a list of what mortgage lenders evaluate when they review your credit report:

- How much you already owe
- How much unused credit you have available
- How prompt you are in paying your debts
- Whether you have recently applied for new credit

The lender may ask you to explain:

- Any late payments
- Recent inquiries on your credit report
- New accounts

If you have no credit accounts, they may ask you to show that you pay your rent, telephone bills or utility payments on time. If your credit score is low, find ways to improve your credit score and rebuild your score.

Have You Saved Enough Money?

To make a major purchase like a house, you generally need to make a down payment. You also need money for closing costs and funds set aside for emergencies. If you spend every dime on your down payment, you're statistically more likely to lose your new home to foreclosure sometime in the future.

Know All Your Options

Ask the lender to give you details on the cost differences among various mortgage plans. Then select the one that's best for you. Here is a breakdown of the typical costs that may be involved in owning a home:

- Mortgage principal
- Property taxes
- Mortgage insurance
- Home insurance
- Special assessments
- Homeowners' Association fees

As a general rule, your housing costs should total no more than 29 percent of your monthly income before taxes. Add other long-term debts, such as car and student loans, and your total should take no more than 36 percent to 41 percent of your monthly income before taxes.

Make Your Payments on Time

How much you borrow, how much you owe and when you pay become a part of your credit report. When you apply for new credit purchases, other lenders will review this history. Late payments can stay on your credit report for up to seven years, can keep you from buying another house or can make it more expensive to buy a car. A good credit history proves that you manage your finances well. It lets you enjoy using credit at your convenience and at a lower cost.

Buying a Car

Reasons to Buy a Car

- You have the money for the down payment that's required for a credit purchase.
- You like the idea of owning something of value after making payments for years.
- You want to trade in an old vehicle.
- You plan to carefully maintain your car so that it runs well for many years.
- You drive tens of thousands of miles each year. If you lease, you might end up paying a relatively large amount of money at the lease's end for exceeding the annual mileage cap, which generally is 12,000 to 15,000 miles.

Reasons to Lease a Car

- You need your cash for other purposes.
- You like driving a new vehicle—perhaps a luxury model—every two or three years.
- You hate the hassle of selling your old car every time you want to buy a new one.
- You drive 15,000 miles or less per year.
- You like the idea of driving a vehicle for a few years before purchasing it.

If you decide to lease, you need to learn exactly what you're paying for in terms of the interest rate. (It should be close to the current automobile loan rate.) You should negotiate the capitalized cost (the price the financial institution pays the dealer for the leased vehicle), the acquisition fee (which the consumer is charged for initiating the lease) and the disposition fee (which the consumer is charged at the lease's end if he or she decides not to buy the vehicle). Because of these factors, professionals advise that low monthly payments don't necessarily translate into a beneficial transaction for the consumer.

When purchasing a vehicle keep in mind the purpose served by the vehicle. Why do you need it and exactly how much can you afford factoring in costs associated with maintenance and insurance. It is generally a good idea to secure financing from a Credit Union or a Bank before going to a dealership. Having pre-arranged financing normally gives you better terms on a loan. The shorter the length of the loan the less money you pay in interest. A vehicle depreciates the second it leaves the lot so it makes much more sense to buy a late model car that is 2 years old that has already depreciated in value.

Buyer Beware

There are car dealers that seek to take advantage of service members. They know service members have a stable income and that if you sign a sales contract that they will get their money even if that means garnishing your wages. A wage garnishment occurs when a court issues an order requiring your employer to withhold a certain amount of your paycheck and send it directly to the person or institution to whom you owe money, until your debt is paid off. In this case your employer would be the Branch of Service that you are a member of (Army/Navy/Air Force/Marines/Coast Guard).

Unfortunately, there are other industries whose business models are built upon overcharging service members and placing them in precarious financial circumstances. It is generally a good idea to check with your command to identify known bad actors and avoid them. It is also a good idea to have someone from your command go with you especially when you are a junior service member when you are making a large purchase/leasing an apartment just to make sure that you are not being taken advantage of.

CHAPTER 8

Money - Trust = Problems

IT IS OFTEN SAID THAT money is one of the most common causes of relationship/marriage difficulty. It is true that couples often have disagreements about money. While money is an issue the real issue is the lack of honest communication about what the money represents. Men and women look at money differently and often have different approaches to managing finances. Problems arise when couples are not honest with one another about their own personal relationship with money. This is what is called financial infidelity.

If a marriage/relationship is going to endure a serious exploration of attitudes regarding money must be held. Questions like are we going to merge all of our accounts? How much are we allowed to spend without consulting the other? How much are we each expected to contribute to household bills? What are our financial aspirations and what are we prepared to do/sacrifice to make reach them? These are the kind of real questions that need to be discussed before forming a household.

People form households but have no idea of how to run a household. Past behavior has to change. You are no longer responsible for yourself only. You have someone else to consider. The decisions that you are making impact someone beside you and that means you may have to change the way you are used to doing things. Maintaining a happy and successful marriage in the military is hard.

Being deployed is hard on each partner and if children are a part of the equation it makes it even tougher to be a functional family in a traditional sense. The service member has to balance the stress that comes with being deployed multiple times in a relatively short period of time. Understanding the need to do your job because the reality is that someone's life often depends on your ability to focus on what you are supposed to be doing and not being distracted by what is happening stateside. Yes, you miss you family, but the best thing you can do is make sure you and everyone you are deployed with come home safely.

The military spouse also has to deal with the stress of not knowing where you are, not knowing what you are doing, and not knowing if you are safe. If this is the first deployment you have made it can be especially hard on the military spouse. They may have had other military spouses share their experiences, but until you have experienced it personally you really do not know what it is like.

Having children makes things easier and more difficult at the same time. It is easier in that you have less time to wonder about the deployed service member because there are children to take care of. You still have to go grocery shopping, make dinner, participate in after school activities, and maintain a household even if one of the parents is not there.

It's harder in that you have to look at your children and try to answer the question of when is Mom/Dad coming home? You have to be calm and confident for them because they are looking to you for cues regarding their behavior. If they see you crying and being visibly upset then that is how they will behave.

The fact remains that military families take care of each other and after a while, the family adapts to the new dynamic. The military spouse takes on added responsibility, and if the children are old enough they take on responsibilities as well. The family evolves and establishes a new normal. The deployed service member becomes a photo or a face on a screen, but not someone to be touched. A child that was a toddler when the deployment started is running and babbling when the service member returns. A significant portion of the child's life was missed and the guilt associated with that can weigh down the service member.

Attempting to reintegrate into a family that has evolved into a functioning unit without you is difficult as you no longer fit in the role you had when you were deployed. How do you discipline a child that may be harboring resentment because you were not there when they needed you? How do you make up for the chunk of their childhood that you missed? The uncomfortable truth is that you cannot. You cannot change the past. What you can do is do the best that you can when you are home.

The guilt experienced by service members may lead to self-destructive or overly permissive behavior as the absent service member may oscillate between self-medicating (i.e. substance or alcohol abuse) and trying to make up for not being there by trying to be a friend instead of being a parent to the children.

The fact is that if you stay in the military long enough, you will be deployed multiple times. The truth is that each time you leave it gets a little bit more difficult to come back. You are hyperaware of your surroundings, you are a much more aggressive driver, and you do not suffer fools well. You are not the same person you were before you left, and how could you be? The friends you have lost and the things you have seen cause you to lose your naivety.

Everyone appreciates your service, but can't seem to understand why you are having a hard time transitioning back into the civilian world. You see individuals that are oblivious to the world that you have left. There are the people who upon learning you served, ask if you killed anybody and if so how many people? There are the people who ask you why do you stay in the military. Everyone has their own reasons for staying, but the fact is you feel a sense of loyalty to the men and women you served with and you don't want to leave them hanging.

It can be difficult to recognize and embrace that you have changed; and you may struggle to figure out how to define a role for yourself in your family. You must learn how to interact with individuals that did not serve in the military. The fact is that less than 1% of the United States population has served or knows someone who has served. That lack of knowledge makes it impossible for them to understand what your service was like.

Facing all of this is exceedingly difficult for some veterans to reintegrate. Far too many service members have been unable to resolve this. While on active duty they had responsibility and respect. They had a purpose and a useful functionality. Separated from service, they find themselves unable to obtain and hold a job that pays a living wage. The resentment and anger builds and they take it out on those closest to them, or self-medicate. Many marriages are not strong enough to deal with the strain.

The End of the Road (Divorce)

Unfortunately, there are times where despite your most sincere efforts it is clear that the marriage has run its course and it is time to go your separate ways. Hopefully, the separation is amiable. But sometimes it is not. In the cases where it is a contested or difficult divorce, you need to be aware of how a divorce may impact your finances and credit.

Divorce and Credit

Your divorce decree does not relieve you from joint debts you incurred while married. You are responsible for joint accounts that range from credit cards and car loans to home mortgages. Even when a divorce judge orders your ex-spouse to pay a certain bill, you're still legally responsible for making sure it is paid because you promised both as a couple and as individuals to do so.

The credit grantor (a bank, credit card issuer, mortgage company or other credit-lending business) also has a legal right to report negative information to a credit reporting company if your ex-spouse pays late on a joint account. If your ex-spouse doesn't pay at all, you'll probably have to pay or the grantor can take legal action against you.

Close or Separate Joint Accounts

Talk to your ex-spouse, if possible. Analyze all your debts and decide who should be responsible for each. Call your creditors and ask them how to transfer your joint accounts to the person who is solely responsible for payments. However, you still might have legal responsibility to pay existing balances unless the creditor agrees to release you from the debt.

Take Stock of Your Properties

You may have to refinance your home to get one name off the mortgage, or you might need to sell your home and divide the proceeds.

Keep Paying All Bills

Until you can separate your accounts, neither of you can afford to miss a turn paying bills. During divorce negotiations, send in at least the minimum payment due on all joint bills. If you miss even one payment and it stays on your credit profile for up to seven years, it makes it hard to obtain new credit in your own name. Beware of well-meaning friends and relatives who may tell you to ignore making payments or to run up debts. Always make all payments with at least the minimum due.

Establish Credit Independently

Start small and build up. Get a credit card that has a small credit limit, perhaps from a local department store or financial institution. Then always pay your bills on time so your credit history will be excellent. After six months, apply for another card and continue paying bills consistently. Don't run your debt up beyond what you can afford to pay. It's a winning strategy that's easy to master.

Ask a family member or friend to cosign. Perhaps a relative or friend with an established credit history can cosign your loan or credit application provided you repay that cosigned debt on time. Remember, any transaction also will show up on the cosigner's credit profile. After a few months, try again to get credit on your own. Consider applying for a secured credit card. You must open and maintain a savings account as security for your line of credit. Your credit line is a percentage of your deposit. Beware of the extra fees you may have to pay for secured credit.

Rebuild a Positive Credit History

You can pick up your pieces and start fresh with a positive credit report; if you pay your bills on time. After all, your credit profile is always evolving. Your recent bill-paying pattern is critical. Your behavior (during the next 18 to 24 months) is most important in deciding whether you're a good credit risk. Even one late payment can affect your ability to get a mortgage.

Help is available if you're having difficulty paying bills. The non-profit National Foundation for Credit Counseling (NFCC), 1 800-388-2227, can help you establish a budget and repay creditors. Other organizations offer quality credit counseling as well. Be sure the organization you work with is non-profit, provides budgeting and financial management training in addition to any debt management plan, and does so at little or no cost. Be very cautious of any organization that claims it can provide a quick fix to your credit problems, provides you with no financial management education, or charges substantial fees for its services.

Bankruptcy is a Last Resort

Bankruptcy should be the last move to make if you get in over your head. It's not an easy way out. Filing for bankruptcy is no guarantee that it will be granted, because a court judgment must be made. Even if all you do is file your bankruptcy papers with the court, it gets reported on your credit profile. Not all debts are included in bankruptcy. Things like alimony, child support, student loans and taxes secured by liens still must be paid consistently.

Bankruptcy remains on your credit history for up to 10 years. While a declaration of bankruptcy removes many debts, any reference to filing, dismissal or discharge still appears on your credit history for up to 10 years. During this time, you'll find it more difficult, and maybe impossible, to get a new mortgage, a personal loan or a credit card.

CHAPTER 9

A Goal Without a Plan

FORMER NFL COACH HERMAN EDWARDS is fond of saying "A goal without a plan is a wish". I'll take that one step further and say if a goal without a plan is a wish then a plan without action is just a dream. I am going to paraphrase Benjamin Franklin and say people do not plan to fail, they simply fail to plan. We think that we always have tomorrow, and think we'll get around to it later. Unfortunately, there comes a time when you are out of tomorrows and you have missed your opportunity.

A life in the military is not forever. There is a very real possibility that you will not be able to retire with twenty or more years of service even if you want to. Your body may fail you. You may be passed over for a promotion one time too many. You may decide to voluntarily separate from the military. The point is that at some point, your service will end. The question is what will you do when it happens?

Referring back to the Powell Doctrine, one of the questions asked, "Is there a plausible exit strategy?" In this challenging economic environment, you have to consider your exit strategy at the beginning rather than the end of your career. If you wait until the end, then your options for equipping yourself with the skills and more importantly the network you need to thrive is limited.

You do not need to know exactly what you want to do for the rest of your life on day 1. You do need to think about what you are interested in. Where do my skills lay and what do I enjoy doing? You are going to need to further your education. It may not be a traditional four-year college degree, but knowledge beyond high school is a necessity in a globally interdependent society. We are not just competing with the best and brightest in America. Your competition happens to be on every continent on the planet. They want what you have and if you don't protect it they will take it.

There are few things sadder than the Senior Staff Non-Commissioned Officer with 18 years of service sitting across from the junior enlisted service member in English Literature class reading Robert Frost and discussing symbolism. The Staff NCO is a proud man, and has the service record to prove it. He also has two bad knees, a herniated disk, 2 failed marriages and kids he doesn't get to see as much as he'd like. Watching this man struggle through class and hearing him say in a tired raspy voice, "Youngblood, don't be like me. I should have done this 15 years ago. You have your whole career ahead of you. Do it right!"

This man has done everything the military has asked and more. He has given of his body and soul. He has served with distinction, but finds himself taking night classes trying to complete a degree before he completes his service. He did not take the steps during the early part of his career to prepare him for transitioning to civilian life. He has learned all of the skills the Military taught him, but the skill he needs most right now is to know how to survive and support himself after separating from the military. Unfortunately, the Military doesn't teach that course.

While education is important, taking steps to place you on a solid financial footing is also important as well. Far too many of those who serve knew little about finances and investments before they joined the military. The sad reality is that they did not learn anything about finances and investments while they were serving as well. This is something service members should focus on early in their careers.

Educational Pursuits

You can take classes while on active duty, but it is difficult to complete a degree while working in your military occupational specialty. Many colleges offer courses in the evening, but any off-duty education opportunities depend on your command allowing you to attend. One of the first things I learned in the Marine Corps was about leadership. The primary objective of Marine Corps leadership is Mission Accomplishment while troop welfare is a secondary consideration.

The harsh and ugly truth is that as members of the uniformed service we are expendable assets. As much as we would like to think of ourselves as important and necessary, the fact is that we can and we will be replaced by someone younger and healthier. Every transitioning service member will be faced with trying to figure out what to do now. If you have not given it any thought, it can be a difficult transition.

Education and networking provides a service member options. You have to be educated and aware as to what opportunities and/or programs you are eligible for. Understanding what your aptitudes are, what environment you are comfortable in, and what physical limitations you have are all important in developing a plan that will allow you to successfully transition to civilian life.

By the time your active duty career is finished you will have hopefully gained more than you have lost. Unfortunately, that is not always the case and if that happens to be your experience then you can apply for benefits from the Veterans Administration (VA):

Applying for Benefits

There are numerous ways to apply for VA benefits depending on the type of benefit you are seeking.

Benefits	How to Apply
Before Leaving Military Service – Pre Discharge Program for Service Members	If you are a member of the armed forces serving on either active duty or full-time National Guard duty, you should apply through the VA Pre-Discharge Program before leaving service.

Benefits	How to Apply
Vocational Rehabilitation and Employment Benefits for Service Members and Veterans	The best way to file for vocational rehabilitation and employment services is to apply online at eBenefits.va.gov. If you don't have a benefits account, register today. In eBenefits, apply using the Veterans On-Line Application (VON-APP) to complete and submit your application online. The form to use is called VA Form 28-1900, "Disabled Veterans Application for Vocational Rehabilitation."

You can also mail the VA Form 28-1900, "Disabled Veterans Application for Vocational Rehabilitation" to your regional benefit office. You can locate your local regional benefit office using the VA Facility Locator. You may also visit your local regional benefit office and turn in your application for processing.

Visit Vocational Rehabilitation and Employment for more information on vocational rehabilitation and employment services |
| Disability Compensation Benefits for Veterans | The best way to file for disability compensation is to apply online at eBenefits.va.gov. If you don't have an eBenefits account, register today. Once you log into your eBenefits account, use Apply for Disability Compensation. VA recommends you appoint an accredited Veterans Service Officer to help you initiate your claim, gather the required medical records and evidence and submit your claim. You can appoint a Veteran Service Officer while you apply online.

If you prefer to file your claim by paper, complete VA Form 21-526EZ, "Application for Disability Compensation and Related Compensation Benefits" and mail the application to your local regional benefit office. You can find an accredited Veteran Service Officer using eBenefits – See www.ebenefits.va.gov/ebenefits/vso-search |

Benefits	How to Apply
Dependency and Indemnity Compensation Benefits for Survivors and Dependents	Download and complete VA Form 21-534EZ, "Application for DIC, Death Pension, and/or Accrued Benefits" and mail it to your local regional benefit office. You may also visit your local regional benefit office and turn in your application for processing.
	We recommend that you appoint an accredited Veterans Service Officer to help you initiate your claim and gather any required medical records or evidence. You can find an accredited Veteran Service Officer using eBenefits – See www.ebenefits.va.gov/ebenefits/vso-search
	Visit Dependency and Indemnity Compensation for more information on compensation benefits for survivors and dependents.
Pension Benefits for Veterans	Download and complete VA Form 21-527EZ, "Application for Pension." You can mail your application to your local regional benefit office and turn in your application for processing.
	VA recommends you appoint an accredited Veterans Service Officer to help you initiate your claim and gather any required medical records or evidence. You can find an accredited Veteran Service Officer using eBenefits.
Pension Benefits for Survivors	Download and complete VA Form 21-534EZ, "Application for DIC, Death Pension, and/or Accrued Benefits" and mail it to your local benefit office. You can locate your local regional benefit office and turn in your application for processing.
	VA recommends you appoint an accredited Veterans Service Officer to help you initiate your claim and gather any required medical records or evidence. You can find an accredited Veteran Service Officer using eBenefits.

Benefits	How to Apply
Education Benefits for Veterans	You can apply for your education benefits using eBenefits.va.gov. If you don't have an eBenefits account, register today. In eBenefits, apply using the Veterans On-line Application (VONAPP) to complete and submit your application online.
	You can also submit a paper application. To do this, download and complete VA Form 22-1990, "Application for VA Educational Benefits" and mail it to a VA Regional Processing Office. You can mail the form to the region of your home address or to the VA Regional Processing Office for the region of your school's physical address, if you know what school you want to attend. Also, you can call a VA Education Case Manager (1-888-GIBill1) to ask for help.
Home Loan Benefits for Service Members and Veterans	You can apply for a home loan certificate of eligibility online using ebenefits.va.gov. You may also apply for a home loan certificate of eligibility through your lender. To apply by mail, use VA Form 26-1880, "Request for Certificate of Eligibility."
	You can mail the application to: VA Loan Eligibility Center Attn: COE (262) PO Box 100034 Decatur, GA 30031
Home Loan Benefits for Survivors	The surviving spouse of a Service Member or Veteran must apply by mail. The form to complete is the VA Form 26-1817, "Request for Determination of Loan Guaranty Eligibility – Unmarried Surviving Spouses." Or, you can call 1-888-768-2132 and follow the prompts for Eligibility and we will mail the form to you.
	Mail your application to this address: VA Loan Eligibility Center Attn: COE (262) PO Box 100034 Decatur, GA 30031

Benefits	How to Apply
Life Insurance Benefits for Service Members, Veterans, and Survivors	Service Members' Group Life Insurance (SGLI): SGLI coverage is automatic. You do not need to apply. To designate beneficiaries, or reduce, decline or restore SGLI coverage, complete and submit SGLV 8286, "Service Members' Group Life Insurance Election and Certificate" to your branch of service personnel clerk.
	Veterans' Group Life Insurance (VGLI): To file for VGLI, you can apply online using eBenefits.va.gov. If you don't have an eBenefits account, register today. You may also download and complete SGLV 8714 "Application for Veterans' Group Life Insurance."
	Mail your application to this address: OSGLI PO Box 41618 Philadelphia, PA 19176-9913
	Family Service Member's Group Life Insurance (FSGLI): To decline, reduce, or restore FSGLI coverage, complete and file form SGLV 8286A, "Spouse Coverage Election and Certificate" with your branch of service.
	Service Member's Group Life Insurance Traumatic Injury Protection Program (TSGLI): To file a claim for TSGLI, complete and file SGLV 8600, "Application for TSGLI Benefits" with your branch of service. Coverage for this benefit is automatic for all Service Members covered by SGLI.
	Service-Disabled Veterans' Insurance (S-DVI): To file for S-DVI, apply online using the online policy access page or complete VA Form 29-4364, "Application for Service-Disabled Veterans' Insurance."
	Mail your application to this address: Department of Veteran Affairs Regional Office and Insurance Center (RH) PO Box 7208 Philadelphia, PA 19101

Benefits	How to Apply
	Veterans' Mortgage Life Insurance (VMLI): To file for VMLI, complete and submit VA Form 29-8636, "Application for Veterans' Mortgage Life Insurance" to your Specially Adapted Housing Agent. The agent will help you complete your application. Also, you must provide information about your current mortgage.

Applying for Benefits and Your Character of Discharge

Generally, in order to receive VA benefits and services, the Veteran's character of discharge of service must be under other than dishonorable conditions (e.g., honorable, under honorable conditions, general). However, individuals receiving undesirable, bad conduct, and other types of dishonorable discharges may qualify for VA benefits depending on a determination made by VA.

Pre-Discharge

Under the Benefits Delivery at Discharge (BDD) an active duty service member may file a claim for disability compensation up to 180 days prior to separation or retirement from active duty or full-time National Guard or Reserve Duty (Titles 10 and 32).

You can apply for disability compensation through one of the following:

- Benefits Delivery at Discharge (BDD)
- Quick Start
- Overseas Intake Sites

	Benefits Delivery at Discharge (BDD)	Quick Start	Overseas Intake Sites
When to apply prior to separation	60 to 180 days	1-59 days	Within 180 days
Availability	Nationwide	Nationwide	Select installations in Germany and Korea

Benefits Delivery at Discharge (BDD)

BDD allows a service member to submit a claim for disability compensation 60 to 180 days prior to separation, retirement, or release from active duty or demobilization. BDD can help you receive VA disability benefits sooner, with a goal of within 60 days after release or discharge.

Eligibility

BDD requires a minimum of 60 days to allow sufficient time to complete the medical examination process (which may involve multiple specialty clinics) prior to separation from service. If you are closer to 60 days to separation from service, you can submit a Quick Start Claim. BDD is available nationwide and open to all service members on full time active duty, including members of the National Guard and Reserve. Members of the Coast Guard may also participate.

Requirements to Participate	BBD Program
Do I have a known separation date?	Yes
How far away is my known separation date?	60 – 180 days
When must I submit my service treatment records to the VA?	At the time claim is submitted
When and where must I complete all phases of my VA/DoD medical separation examination process?	At your point of separation, prior to release from the military
When may I apply?	If you meet all of the BDD requirements above, you may apply for BDD 60-180 days prior to separation

How to Apply

To file a pre-discharge claim under BDD, do one of the following:

- Submit your application online using eBenefits and follow the instructions about where to submit your service treatment records.

- Complete the VA Form 21-526EZ (See PDF), Application for Disability Compensation and Related Compensation Benefits, and submit it with copies of your service treatment records to the VA location nearest you.
- Call VA toll free at 1-800-827-1000 to have the claim form mailed to you.
- Visit your local VA regional office. For the VA regional office nearest you, call VA toll-free at 1-800-827-1000

For more Information

If you are on a military installation, contact your local Transition Assistance Office or ACAP Center (Army only) to schedule appointments to attend VA benefits briefings and learn how to initiate your claim. You can also call the VA toll-free at 1-800-827-1000.

Quick Start Program

Quick Start allows a service member to submit a claim for disability compensation 1 to 59 days prior to separation, retirement, or release from active duty or demobilization. Submitting your disability compensation claim before discharge makes it possible to receive VA disability benefits as soon as possible after separation, retirement, or demobilization.

Eligibility

Service members with 1-59 days remaining on active duty or full time Reserve or National Guard (Title 10 or Title 32) service, or service members who do not meet the Benefits Delivery at Discharge (BDD) criteria requiring availability for all examinations prior to discharge, may apply through Quick Start. The program is available nationwide and open to all service members on full active duty including members of the National Guard and Reserves.

Requirements to Participate	Quick Start Program
Do I have a known separation date?	Yes
How far away is my known separation date?	1 – 59 days
When must I submit my service treatment records to VA	At the time the claim submitted
When and where must I complete all phases of my VA/Dodd medical separation examination process?	At your point of separation, prior to release from the military
When may I apply?	If you meet all of the requirements above, you may apply for Quick Start 1-59 days prior to separation. *Quick Start allows National Guard or Reserve members attending demobilization briefings to file a claim and leave the area where the VA disability claim was submitted. Those unable to complete the application before separation can submit a claim through the traditional claims process after separation

How to Apply

To file a pre-discharge claim under Quick Start, do one of the following:

- Submit your application online using eBenefits and follow the instructions about where to submit your service treatment records.
- Complete the VA Form 21-526EZ (See PDF), Application for Disability Compensation and Related Compensation Benefits, and submit it with copies of your service treatment records to the VA location nearest you.
- Call VA toll free at 1-800-827-1000 to have the claim form mailed to you
- Visit your local VA regional office. For the VA regional office nearest you, call VA toll-free at 1-800-827-1000

For More Information

If you are on a military installation, contact your local Transition Assistance Office or ACAP Center (Army only) to schedule appointments to attend VA benefits briefings and learn how to initiate your claim. You can also call the VA toll-free at 1-800-827-1000.

Overseas Intake Sites

*   Germany
*   Korea

Germany

Benefits Delivery at Discharge (BDD) Office
Landstuhl Regional Medical Center
Building 3700 – Room 214
Phone: DSN 486-8028 or CIV 06371-86-8028
(0049-6371-86-8028) Outside Germany
Fax: DSN 486-7886 or CIV 06371-86-7886
(0049-6371-86-7886) Outside Germany
Email: GermanyBDD.vbapit@va.gov

The Benefits Delivery at Discharge (BDD) Office in Landstuhl, Germany, accepts pre-discharge claims from active-duty service members stationed in Europe, Africa and the Middle East. Service members must be within 180 days of their effective separation or retirement date and be able to schedule and report to all necessary examinations at LRMC.

Service members stationed within the Kaisersalutern Military Community (KMC) should visit the Landstuhl BDD Office and submit their application package (VA Form 21-526, service treatment records) in person. Walk-in hours are from Tuesday through Thursday 10:00 to 12:00 and 13:00 to 15:00 hours.

Service members stationed outside the KMC, can participate in the BDD or Quick Start programs through the "Fly-in" claim process.

The Fly-in claim process reduces the necessary travel by allowing service members to submit applications by fax or e-mail. Participants are required to make just one trip to Landstuhl to complete a physical examination.

To Participate in the Fly-in claim process:

1. Contact the Landstuhl BDD Office, by phone, fax or email.
Service members will then be provided with all the necessary information and forms via email.

2. Complete and return the application.
After the BDD office receives the necessary paperwork, the service member will be contacted via email with instructions to schedule examinations at LRMC. Notification about what information and evidence is needed to support the claim will be provided via email.

3. Schedule and report for necessary examinations at LRMC.
Service members will contact the clinics to schedule the necessary exams as directed in the instructions provided. Travel to Landstuhl must be arranged by the service member and approved by his or her command.

4. Submit service treatment records (STRs) to VA.
When service members report for the physical, they must bring a copy of their STRs which will be submitted to VA and not be returned. BDD and Quick Start Claims can not be processed without the STRs.

Korea
Benefits Delivery Discharge (BDD) claims can be filed on a walk-in basis or by calling DSN 738-5121 to schedule an appointment.
VA staff will schedule individual assistance sessions to file BBD claims at:

United States Army Garrison (USAG) Yongsan (738-7334/7322)
USAG Camp Casey (730-4033/4044)
USAG Camp Humphries (753-8839)
Osan Air Force Base (784-5440)

To be eligible for the BDD program, service members must have time available to attend exams prior to departing Korea. Retiring and separating service members should contact the Soldier for Life TAP (SFL-TAP) or the Airman Family and Readiness Center at DSN: 315-784-05440; commercial: 011-82-31-661-5440 or email osan.afrc@us.af.mil for the BDD visitation schedule.

The BDD office also provides assistance to veterans, retirees, widows, or dependents residing in-country regarding VA benefit entitlements, claims for increase, new or reopened claims for compensation or pension benefits, and appeals.

Integrated Disability Evaluation System

The "Integrated Disability Evaluation System (IDES) Examination Templates page" is used to determine a service member's fitness for duty. The Departments of Defense (DoD) and Veterans Affairs (VA) worked together to make disability evaluation seamless, simple, fast and fair. If the service member is found medically unfit for duty, the IDES gives them a proposed VA disability rating before they leave the service.

For more Information

While in a pre-discharge program, you may also apply for other VA benefits, such as Vocational Rehabilitation and Employment, Education, and Loan Guaranty. The following resources are available when initially applying for benefits:

- Visit VA Returning Service Members (OEF/OIF) – www.oefoif. va.gov and Seamless Transition –www.benefits.va.gov/VOW/

tap.asp for additional information, including resources for family and outreach activities for returning service members.

- The Summary of VA Benefits (See PDF – www.benefits.va.gov/BENEFITS/benefits-summary/SummaryofVABenefitsFlyer.pdf) is a printable brochure that provides at-a-glance description of VA benefits.
- Visit DoD TAP – www.dodtap.mil and Military One Source – www.militaryonesource.mil for 24/7 access to helpful guides on pre-separation and transition, information on employment, education, relocation, benefits and more.

Claims Based on Post-Service: Diseases after Service

Veterans with service-related disabilities that appear after they have ben discharged may still be eligible for disability compensation. An overview of these types of compensation are described below:

Agent Orange

The VA presumes that if you served in Vietnam or in or near the Korean demilitarized zones, during certain time periods, you were exposed to Agent Orange. Veterans with this service who also have a disease related to Agent Orange exposure may be eligible for disability compensation. Veterans who have a disease associated with Agent Orange, but do not meet the service requirements for the VA to "presume" actual exposure to Agent Orange must show an actual connection between the disease and the herbicide exposure during military service.

Disabilities that Appear within One Year after Discharge

Veterans with certain diseases that presented themselves after discharge from military service may be eligible for disability compensation. This includes certain diseases that were not incurred in or aggravated by military service, but which VA presumes are related to military service if shown to exist within a certain time period after service. Examples include: hypertension, arthritis, diabetes mellitus, and peptic ulcers. A complete list of disease is in Title 38, Code of Federal Regulation, 3.309(a)

Eligibility Requirements

- You must be a Veteran who was discharged under conditions other than dishonorable.
- You must have a disease that is at least 10% disabling within one year after separation from service.
- The disease must be among those listed in Title 38, Code of Federal Regulation (See Word Document).

Exception: The requirement that the disease must have appeared within one year of separation from service does not apply to the following:

- Hansen's Disease must have appeared within three years of separation.
- Tuberculosis must have appeared within three years of separation.
- Multiple Sclerosis (MS) must have appeared within seven years of separation.
- Amyotrophic Lateral Sclerosis (ALS), also known as Lou Gehrig's Disease any time after separation from service

Evidence Requirements

- The evidence must show that the disease is at least 10 percent disabling. (An example is you're taking medication for hypertension).
- The evidence must show the disease appeared within the time limits shown above.

How to Apply

- Apply online using eBenefits,
- Work with an accredited representative or agent,
- Go to a VA regional office and have a VA employee assist you. You can find your regional office on our Facility Locator page. (Insert list of regional office/Map with Office location)

Exposure to Hazardous Materials

Veterans may have been exposed to a range of chemical, physical and environmental hazards during military service. Veterans may be entitled to disability compensation if exposure to these hazards resulted in a disease or injury. Examples include exposure to radiation, mustard gas, and asbestos.

Asbestos

If you served in any of the following military occupation specialties, you may have been exposed to asbestos: mining, milling, shipyard work, insulation work, demolition of old buildings, carpentry, construction, or manufacturing and installation of products such as flooring and roofing. Additionally, if you served in Iraq or other countries in that region, you could have been exposed to asbestos when older buildings were damaged and the contaminant was released in the air.

Contaminated Drinking Water at Camp Lejeune

Water systems at Marine Corps Base in Lejeune, NC were contaminated with chemical compounds from at least 1957 to February 1985 when the wells supplying the water systems were shut down. These water systems served housing, administrative, and recreational facilities, as well as the base hospital. There is limited and suggestive evidence of an association between certain diseases and the chemical compounds found at Camp Lejeune during the period of contamination.

Specific Environmental Hazards

You may have been exposed to environmental hazards at military installations during military service. These hazards include:

- Burn Pits
- Particulate Matter
- Chemical Fires
- Waste Disposal Pollution

Ionizing Radiation

Veterans may have been exposed to ionizing radiation during military service if, for example, they participated in nuclear weapons testing. There are certain diseases that may be service-connected if the disease occurred as a result of the radiation exposure.

Mustard Gas

Approximately 4,500 service members were exposed to "mustard gas" as "volunteer soldier" subjects for experiments conducted by the Department of Defense. This exposure may result in health problems.

Gulf War Illnesses

Gulf War Veterans suffering from what is commonly referred to as "Gulf War Syndrome", which is a cluster of medically unexplained chronic symptoms that can include fatigue, headaches, joint pain, indigestion, insomnia, dizziness, respiratory disorders and memory problems may be eligible for disability compensation. In addition, Gulf War Veterans who served in Southwest Asia and have a disability resulting from certain infectious diseases may be eligible for disability compensation.

Prisoners of War (POWs)

VA presumes that certain medical conditions are associated with a Former POW's captivity. If you are a former POW who has been diagnosed as having one or more of these conditions to a degree that is at least 10% disabling, VA presumes that it is associated with the POW experience and you are entitled to disability compensation.

Special Claims

Compensation is not always based on an in-service event. Additionally, other benefits may be available after disability compensation has been awarded. An overview of these VA benefits is provided below.

Title 38 U.S.C. 1151 Claims

VA may provide compensation for injuries incurred or aggravated while receiving care from the VA, such as medical treatment or vocational rehabilitation.

Automobile Allowance

VA may provide Veterans with a one-time allowance to purchase a new or used car to accommodate a service-connected disability. This benefit is available to Veterans with certain service-connected disabilities, such as the loss of or permanent loss of use of a hand or foot. This benefit can also be used to purchase adaptive equipment.

Birth Defects/Spina Bifida

VA may provide a tax-free monetary allowance to children with Spina Bifida or certain birth defects born to women who served in the Republic of Vietnam or served in or near the demilitarization zone in Korea during certain time periods.

Clothing Allowance

VA may provide an annual clothing allowance to Veterans who use a prosthetic or orthopedic device (including a wheelchair) because of a service-connected disability, or have a service-connected skin condition and us a medication that causes irreparable damage to outer garments.

Convalescence

VA may grant a temporary 100 percent disability compensation rating to recover from surgery or immobilization of a joint by a cast without surgery for a service-connected disability.

Dentistry

Dental benefits are provided by the Department of Veterans Affairs (VA) according to law. In some instances, VA is authorized to provide extensive dental care, while in other cases treatment may be limited.

Hospitalization

VA may grant a temporary 100 percent disability compensation rating to a Veteran who is hospitalized for more than 21 days for a service-connected disability.

Individual Non-employability

VA may pay disability compensation at the 100 percent rate to certain Veterans who are unable to maintain substantially gainful employment as a result of service-connected disabilities, even though VA has not rated their service-connected disabilities at the total level.

Pre-stabilization

VA may grant a temporary 12-month 50 percent or 100 percent initial rating to a Veteran who recently separated from service and has an unstable disability and is in need and cannot be self-sufficient.

CHAPTER 10

Health Benefits

Veterans Eligibility

For VA health benefits and services, a person who has served in the active military service and who was discharged or released under conditions other than dishonorable is a Veteran.

Basic Eligibility

If you served in the active service military and were separated under any condition other than dishonorable, you may qualify for VA health care benefits. Current and former members of the Reserves or National Guard who were called to active duty by a federal order and completed the full period for which they were called or ordered to active duty may be eligible for VA health benefits as well. Note: Reserves or National Guard members with active duty for training purposes only do not meet the basic eligibility requirement.

Minimum Duty Requirements

Most Veterans who enlisted after September 7, 1980, or entered active duty after October 16, 1981, must have served 24 continuous months or the full period for which they were called to active duty in order to be eligible. This minimum requirement may not apply to Veterans who were discharged for a disability incurred or aggravated in the line of duty, for a hardship or "early out," or those who served prior to September 7,

1980. Since there are a number of other exceptions to the minimum duty requirements, VA encourages all Veterans to apply so that we may determine their enrollment eligibility.

Enhanced Eligibility

Certain Veterans may be afforded enhanced eligibility status when applying and enrolling in the VA health care system. Veterans who:

- Are a Former Prisoner of War (POW)
- In receipt of the Purple Heart Medal
- In receipt of the Medal of Honor
- Have a compensable VA awarded service-connected disability of 10% or more
- In receipt of a VA pension
- Were discharged from the military because of a disability (not pre-existing), early out or hardship
- Served in Theater of Operations for 5 years post discharge
- Served in the Republic of Vietnam from January 9, 1962 to May 7, 1975 – US Navy and Coast Guard ships associated with military service in Vietnam
- Served in the Persian Gulf from August 2, 1990 to November 11, 1998
- Were stationed or resided at Camp Lejeune for 30 days or more between August 1, 1953 and December 31, 1987
- Are found by the VA to be catastrophically disabled
- Previous years' household income is below VA's National Income or Geographical-Adjusted Thresholds

Enrollment

VA operates an annual enrollment system that helps to maintain the provision of health care. VA applies a variety of factors during the application verification process when determining a Veterans' eligibility for enrollment, but once a Veteran is enrolled, that Veteran remains enrolled in the VA health care system and maintains access to certain VA health benefits.

Cancelling Enrollment

You may request to disenroll from VA Health Care, commonly referred to as cancel/decline, at any time. To request to be disenrolled, you must submit a signed and dated document requesting to be disenrolled from VA health care to a VA Medical Center or you may mail the request to:

VA Health Eligibility Center (HEC)
2957 Clairmont Road
Atlanta, GA 30329

If you decide to cancel your VA health care coverage, please note this may impact your health care coverage requirements under the Affordable Care Act if you do not have other qualifying health care. You may reapply for enrollment at any time by completing a new VA Form 10-10EZ, Application for Health Benefits online at www.va.gov/healthbenefits/enroll, by calling 1-877-222-VETS (8387) or by visiting your local VA health care facility. Please note that you will be considered a new applicant and eligibility for enrollment will be based upon eligibility requirements in place at that time.

Priority Groups

The number of Veterans who can be enrolled in the health care program is determined by the amount of money Congress gives the VA each year. Since funds are limited, VA set up Priority Groups to make sure that certain groups of Veterans are able to enroll before others.

Once you apply for enrollment, your eligibility will be verified. Based on your specific eligibility status, you will be assigned a Priority Group. The Priority Groups range from 1-8 with 1 being the highest priority for enrollment. Based on eligibility and income, some Veterans may have to agree to pay copay to be placed in certain Priority Groups and some Veterans may not be eligible for enrollment.

You may be eligible for more than one Enrollment Priority Group. In that case, VA will place you in the highest Priority Group that you are eligible for. Under the Medical Benefits Package, the same services are generally available to all enrolled Veterans. VA determines your eligibility for VA's comprehensive medical benefits package through the patient enrollment system, which is based on Priority Groups 1 through 8.

Priority Group 1

- Veterans with VA-rated service-connected disabilities 50% or more disabling
- Veterans determined by VA to be unemployable due to service-connected conditions

Priority Group 2

- Veterans with VA-rated service-connected disabilities 30% to 40% disabling

Priority Group 3

- Veterans who are former Prisoners of War (POWs)
- Veterans awarded a Purple Heart medal
- Veterans whose discharge was for a disability that was incurred or aggravated in the line of duty
- Veterans with VA-rated service-connected disabilities 10% or 20% disabled

- Veterans awarded special eligibility classification under Title 38, U.S.C., § 1151, "benefits for individuals disabled by treatment or vocational rehabilitation"
- Veterans awarded the Medal Of Honor (MOH)

Priority Group 4

- Veterans who are receiving aid and attendance or housebound benefits from VA
- Veterans who have been determined by VA to be catastrophically disabled

Priority Group 5

- Nonservice-connected Veterans and non-compensable service-connected Veterans rated 0% disabled by VA with annual income below the VA's and geographically (based on your resident zip code) adjusted income limits.
- Veterans receiving VA pension benefits
- Veterans eligible for Medicaid programs

Priority Group 6

- Compensable 0% service-connected Veterans
- Veterans exposed to Ionizing Radiation during atmospheric testing or during the occupation of Hiroshima and Nagasaki
- Project 112/SHAD participants
- Veterans who served in the Republic of Vietnam between January 9, 1962 and May 7, 1975
- Veterans of the Persian Gulf War who served between August 2, 1990 and November 11, 1998

- *Veterans who served on active duty at Camp Lejeune for not fewer than 30 days beginning August 1, 1953 and ending December 31, 1987
- Veterans who served in a theater of combat operations after November 11, 1998 as follows:
- Currently enrolled Veterans and new enrollees who were discharged from active duty on or after January 28, 2003, are eligible for the enhanced benefits for 5 years post discharge.
- Combat Veterans who were discharged between January 2009 and January 2011, and did not enroll in VA health care during their 5 year period of eligibility have an additional one year to enroll and receive care. The additional one year eligibility period began February 12, 2015 with the signing of the Clay Hunt Suicide Prevention for American Veterans Act

Note: At the end of this enhanced enrollment priority group placement time period Veterans will be assigned the highest Priority Group their unique eligibility status at the time qualifies for.

*Note: While eligible for Priority Group (PG) 6, until system changes are implemented you would be assigned to PG 7 or 8 depending on your income.

Priority Group 7

- Veterans with gross household income below the geographically-adjusted income limits (GMT) for their resident location and who agree to pay copays.

Priority Group 8

- Veterans with gross household income above the VA and the geographically-adjusted income limits for their resident location and who agree to pay copays.

Veterans <u>eligible</u> for enrollment:
Non-compensable 0% service-connected:

- <u>Sub-priority a:</u> Enrolled as of January 16, 2003, and who have remained enrolled since that date and/or placed in this sub priority due to changed eligibility status.
- <u>Sub-priority b:</u> Enrolled on or after June 15, 2009 whose income exceeds the current VA or geographic income limits by 10% or less.

Nonservice-connected and:

- <u>Sub-priority c:</u> Enrolled as of January 16, 2003, and who have remained enrolled since that date and/or placed in this sub priority due to changed eligibility status.
- <u>Sub-priority d:</u> Enrolled on or after June 15, 2009 whose income exceeds the current VA or geographic income limits by 10% or less.

Veterans <u>not eligible</u> for enrollment:
Veterans not meeting the criteria above:

- Sub-priority e: Non-compensable 0% service-connected (eligible for care of their SC condition only)
- Sub-priority g: Nonservice-connected

Active Duty Service Members

Active duty service members who have received their separation and/ or retirement orders may apply for enrollment in the VA health care system. If eligible, service members become enrolled upon separation or retirement.

Transitioning from TRICARE to Veteran's Health Benefits

When service members leave active duty, they may be eligible for benefits offered by TRICARE and the VA, depending on whether they retire or how they separate from the military. If retiring, a service member is eligible for TRICARE as a military retiree and may be eligible for certain VA benefits. Service members who separate due to a service-connected disease or injury may be eligible for VA health benefits and certain TRICARE benefits.

Operation Enduring Freedom (OEF), Operation Iraqi Freedom (OIF) and Operation New Dawn (OND) combat Veterans can receive cost free medical care for any condition related to their service in the Iraq/Afghanistan theater for five years after the date of their discharge or release. In order to take advantage of these benefits, OEF, OIF and OND Vets need to enroll in VA's health care system. Apply online using VA Form 10-10EZ, Application for Health Benefits (See PDF) – www.1010ez.med.va.gov.

A service member in the process of being medically retired can find out if he or she qualifies for VA health benefits for a service-connected injury by consulting with a VA benefit counselor. The VA benefit counselor will assist them in submitting a health benefits application and determining what their military and VA medical board ratings mean with respect to health care coverage. Veterans who qualify for VA health benefits usually receive care for their service-connected injuries at the VA.

Although medically-retired Veterans receive care for their service-connected disability at the VA, they may be eligible to receive all other care through TRICARE. Under their TRICARE benefits, they may have a choice between TRICARE Prime, Standard and Extra. Their eligible family members are also afforded the same options. To learn more about transitioning to VA health benefits, contact VA at 1-877-222-VETS or visit the TRICARE to VA website – www.tricare.mil/tricaretova.

Utilizing VA Medical Services while on Active Duty

Active Duty Service Members

Under certain circumstances, active duty service members may receive limited health benefits and health care services at VA medical centers through sharing agreements. VHA health care services are provided to Active Duty and Reserve Component (RC) Service Members under the following circumstances:

Emergent or Urgent Care

VA always treats active duty Service Members needing urgent or emergent medical care first and seeks authorization once the active duty Service Member has been stabilized.

Routine

VA will only provide routine care to Active Duty Service Members with a valid TRICARE referral or authorization.

VA/DOD Sharing Agreement

Certain locations have sharing agreements that allow certain services to be performed without referrals. Contact your local Military Treating Facility (MTF) or TRICARE office for more information.

CHAPTER 11

VA Compensation

Claims Process

There are eight distinct steps that most claims for disability compensation follow. These phases may vary in time depending on the complexity of the claim, the amount of evidence that must be gathered to support the claims, and the type of evidence. You are strongly encouraged to submit as much evidence as possible with your claim to help minimize processing time. The eight steps of claims processing are as follows:

Step 1 – Claim Received

Your claim has been received by the VA. If you applied online with VONAPP Direct Connect, you should see the receipt in your list of Open Claims within one hour. If you applied through U.S. mail, please allow mailing time plus one week for us to process and record the receipt of your claim.

Step 2 – Under Review

Your claim has been assigned to a Veterans Service Representative and is being reviewed to determine if additional evidence is needed. If we do not need any additional information, your claim will move directly to the "Preparation for Decision" phase.

Step 3 – Gathering of Evidence

The Veterans Service Representative will request evidence from the required sources. Requests for evidence may be made of you, a medical professional, a government agency, or another authority. It is common for claims to return to this phase should additional evidence be required.

Step 4 – Review of Evidence

We have received all needed evidence. If, upon review, it is determined that more evidence is required, the claim will be sent back to the "Gathering of Evidence" phase.

Step 5 – Preparation for Decision

The Veterans Service Representative has recommended a decision, and is preparing required documents detailing that decision. If more evidence is required, the claim will be sent back into the process for more information or evidence.

Step 6 – Pending Decision Approval

The recommended decision is reviewed, and a final award approval is made. If it is determined that more evidence or information is required, the claim will be sent back into the process for more information or evidence.

Step 7 – Preparation for Notification

Your entire claim decision packet is prepared for mailing.

Step 8 – Complete

The VA has sent a decision packet to you by U.S. mail. The packet includes details of the decision or award. Please allow standard mailing time for your packet to arrive before contacting a VA call center.

How Long will this Process Take?

The length of time it takes to complete a claim depends on several factors, such as the type of claim filed, complexity of your disability(ies), the number of disabilities you claim, and the availability of evidence needed to decide your claim. You can track the status of your claim by registering for eBenefits at www.ebenefits.va.gov. You can also visit VA's ASPIRE web site atwww.benefits.va.gov/reports/aspire.asp. Here, you can find the average processing days for the regional office that is working on your claim. To find the average processing days for your state:

- Find your state on the map, place your cursor on the state and click.
- This will open the Veterans Benefits Administration Aspire – Benefits site. Click "Enter".
- You should see a split table. On the left table click on "Compensation".
- This will expand the table. Approximately five rows down is "Rating Claims Processing Time".
- Follow that row to the right until you locate the cell located within the column of your regional office.

The number you see is the average processing days to complete a claim that requires a disability rating. The average is based on completed claims since October 1 in a given fiscal year.

Fully Developed Claims

What Is a Fully Developed Claim?

The Fully Developed Claims (FDC) program is an optional initiative that offers Veterans and survivors faster decisions from the VA on compensation, pension, and survivor benefit claims. Veterans and survivors simply submit all relevant records in their possession, and those records which are easily obtainable, such as private medical records at the time they file their claim and certify that they have no further evidence to submit. The VA can then review and process the claim more quickly.

Many Types of Claims

There are many types of claims for disability compensation. For example, if you're filing a VA claim for the very first time, you have an original claim. A reopened claim means you have new and material evidence and you want the VA to reconsider a claim that was once denied. There are new claims, secondary claims and special claims. To learn more about which type of claim you may have and the evidence and forms you need with you submission, view the Claim and Evidence page – www.benefits.va.gov/FDC/checklist.asp. Your claim must meet all the applicable requirements listed to be considered for the FDC program.

Who Can File an FDC?

Veterans may file an FDC for disability compensation for the following reasons:

- An injury, disability, or condition believed to have occurred or been aggravated by military service
- A condition caused or aggravated by an existing service-related condition

Veterans and their families and survivors may also file pension or dependency and indemnity compensation (survivor) claims at these pages:

- File an FDC: Survivor Benefits
- File an FDC: Pension

Why use the FDC Process?

FDC puts you in control, and it's faster and risk-free.

By filing an FDC, Veterans and survivors take charge of their claim by providing all the evidence at once. By certifying that there is no more evidence, VA can issue a decision faster. File an FDC without risk. Participation will not affect the attention your claim receives from qualified VA rating staff or the benefits to which you are entitled.

If the VA determines other non-federal records exist and are required to decide a claim, VA will simply remove the claim from the FDC program and process it through the traditional claims process. Once you initiate your FDC, you'll have up to one year to complete it. Should VA approve your claim, you'll be paid back to the day you initiated your claim.

What's the Best Way to File an FDC?

- The best way to file an FDC is electronically at eBenefits.va.gov. Once you log in to your account, VA recommends you appoint an accredited Veterans Service Officer to help you initiate your claim, gather the required medical records and evidence, and submit your claim.
- If you prefer to file your FDC by paper, complete VA Form 21-526EZ (See the PDF) and visit your local regional office. You can appoint an accredited Veterans Service Officer to help you prepare and submit your claim. You can also appoint your accredited Veterans Service Officer online at eBenefits.va.gov.

How Should I Prepare My FDC?

- Register for an eBenefits.va.gov account.
- Appoint an accredited Veterans Service Officer who can provide free, expert assistance.

- Gather relevant documents, such as private medical records. While the VA will obtain Federal records on your behalf, such as your DD-214 or service medical records, submitting them if you have them will save time. If you believe there is not a notation in your service record describing your disability, submit a letter from friends or those you have served with that describe the facts of your claim.
- Initiate your claim on eBenefits.va.gov or call 1-800-827-1000 for assistance.

Effective Dates

When VA makes a determination that a compensation award is to be paid based on a claim, an effective date is also assigned. The effective date determines when benefits are payable. Effective dates can vary based on the type of benefit and the circumstances of the claim.

How Effective Dates are Assigned

Listed below are the most common types of claims and generally how effective dates are assigned for each type.

Direct Service-Connection

Generally, an effective date for service-connection for a disability that is directly linked to an injury or disease that was incurred or aggravated by military service is the date VA receives a claim or the date entitlement arose, which ever is later. The date entitlement arose means the date the condition was shown to exist by medical evidence. There is an exception in cases where the claim is filed within one year of separation from active military service. For these claims, the effective date will be the day following separation.

Presumptive Service-Connection

Generally, an effective date for service-connection for a disability that is presumed to be related to military service is the date entitlement arose if the claim is received by the VA within one year of release from active duty. If the claim is received by VA after one year of released from active duty, the effective date is the date of receipt of the claim or the date entitlement arose, whichever is later.

Reopened Claims

Normally, the effective date for a reopened claim is the date of receipt of claim or date entitlement arose, which ever is later.

Liberalizing Law Change

If there is a change in law or VA regulation that allows for VA to pay disability compensation, the effective date may be assigned in the following ways:

- If a claim is reviewed on the initiative of the VA within 1 year from the effective date of the law or VA regulation, or the request of a claimant is received within 1 year from the date of the change in law or regulation.
- If more than one year has elapsed since the change in law or regulation, an effective date of one year prior to either VA's own review or one year prior to the claimant's request for review may be assigned as the effective date.

Dependency and Indemnity Compensation

For claims based on death in service, the effective date will be the first day of the month in which the death actually or was presumed to have occurred.

- If the death occurred after service and the claim is received within one year of the Veteran's death, the effective date will be the first day of the month in which the Veteran died.

- If the death occurred after service and the claim is received after one year of the Veteran's death, the effective date is the date of receipt of claim.

Error

If the VA finds an error in a previous decision, the effective date of the new decision will be the date from which benefits would have been payable had their not been an error.

Increases

The earliest date as of which it is factually ascertainable that an increase in disability had occurred if the claim is received within 1 year from such date, otherwise, the date the claim was received.

Disability of Death Due to Hospitalization

- Disability – Date the injury or aggravation was suffered if claim is received within 1 year after that date; otherwise, the date the claim was received
- Death – First day of month in which the Veteran's death occurred, if a claim is received within 1 year following the date of death; otherwise, the date the claim was received

CHAPTER 12

VA Home Loans

About Home Loans

VA helps service members, Veterans and eligible surviving spouses become homeowners. As part of our mission to serve you, we provide a home loan guaranty benefit and other housing-related programs to help you buy, build, repair or adapt a home for your own personal occupancy. VA home loans are provided by private lenders such as banks and mortgage companies. VA guarantees a portion of the loan, enabling the lender to provide you with more favorable terms.

Purchase and Cash-Out Refinance Home Loans

With a *Purchase Loan*, the VA can help you purchase a home at a competitive interest rate, and if you have found it difficult to find other financing.

VA's *Cash-Out Refinance Loan* is for homeowners who want to take cash out of your home equity to take care of concerns like paying off debt, funding school, or making home improvements. The Cash-Out Refinance Loan can also be used to refinance a non-VA loan into a VA loan. VA will guarantee loans up to 100% of the value of your home.

About the VA Home Loan Guarantee

Most VA Home Loans handled entirely by private lenders and VA rarely gets involved in the loan approval process. VA "stands behind" the loan by guaranteeing a portion of it. If something goes wrong and you can't make the payments anymore, the lending institution can come to us to cover any losses that may occur. The VA loan is the "insurance" that we provide the lender.

VA Home Loan Advantages

The guarantee VA provides to lenders allows them to provide you with more favorable terms, including:

- No down payment as long as the sales price does not exceed the appraised value
- No private mortgage insurance premium requirement
- VA rules limit the amount you can be charged for closing costs
- Closing costs may be paid by the seller.
- The lender can't charge you a penalty fee if you pay the loan off early.
- VA may be able to provide you assistance if you run into difficulty making payments.

You should know that:

- You don't have to be a first-time homebuyer.
- You can reuse the benefit.
- VA-backed loans are assumable, as long as the person assuming the loan qualifies.

Eligibility

You must have suitable credit, sufficient income and a valid Certificate of Eligibility (COE) to be eligible for a VA-guaranteed home loan. The home must be for your own personal occupancy. The eligibility requirements to obtain a COE are listed below for Service members and Veterans, spouses and other eligible beneficiaries.

VA home loans can be used to:

- Buy a home, a condominium unit in a VA-approved project
- Build a home
- Simultaneously purchase and improve a home
- Improve a home by installing energy-related features or making energy efficient improvements
- Buy a manufactured home and/or lot

Eligibility Requirements for VA Home Loans

Status	Qualifying Wartime and Peacetime Periods	Qualifying Active Duty Dates	Minimum Active Duty Service Requirement
Veteran	WWII	9/16/1940 – 7/25/1947	90 total days
	Post-WWII	7/26/1947 – 6/26/1950	181 continuous days
	Korean War	6/27/1950 – 1/31/1955	90 total days
	Post-Korean War	2/1/1955 – 8/4/1964	181 continuous days
	Vietnam War	8/5/1964 – 5/7/1975 *For Veterans who served in the Republic of Vietnam, the beginning date is 2/28/1961	90 total days
	Post-Vietnam War	5/8/1975 – 9/7/1980 *The ending date for officers is 10/16/1981	181 continuous days
	24-Month Rule	9/8/1980 – 8/1/1990 *The beginning date for officers is 10/17/1981	24 continuous months, OR the full period (at least 181 days) for which you were called or ordered to active duty

Status	Qualifying Wartime and Peacetime Periods	Qualifying Active Duty Dates	Minimum Active Duty Service Requirement
	Gulf War	8/2/1990 – Present	24 continuous months, OR the full period (at least 90 days) for which you were called or ordered to active duty
Currently On Active Duty	Any	Any	90 continuous days
National Guard & Reserve Member	Gulf War	8/2/1990 – Present	90 days active service
	Six years of service in the Selected Reserve or National Guard, AND • Were discharged honorably, OR • Were placed on the retired list, OR • Were transferred to the Standby Reserve or an element of the Ready Reserve other than the Selected Reserve after service characterized as honorable, OR • Continue to serve in the Selected Reserve		

*If you do not meet the minimum service requirements, you may still be eligible if you were discharged due to (1) hardship, (2) the convenience of the government, (3) reduction-in-force, (4) certain medical conditions, or (5) a service-connected disability.

Spouses

The spouse of a Veteran can also apply for home loan eligibility under one of the following conditions:

- Un-remarried spouse of a Veteran who dies while in service or from a service connected disability.
- The spouse of a service member missing in action or a prisoner of war
- Surviving spouse who remarries on or after attaining 57, and on or after December 16, 2003

(Note: a surviving spouse who remarried before December 16, 2003, and on or after attaining age 57, must have applied no later than December 15, 2004, to establish home loan eligibility. VA must deny applications from surviving spouses who remarried before December 6, 2003 that are received after December 15, 2004.)

- Surviving spouses of certain totally disabled veterans whose disability may not have been the cause of death

Other Eligible Beneficiaries

You may also apply for eligibility if you fall into one of the following categories:

- Certain U.S. citizens who served in the armed forces of a government allied with the United States in World War II
- Individuals with service in certain organizations, such as Public Health Service officers, cadets at the United States Military, Air Force or Coast Guard Academy, midshipmen at the United States Naval Academy, officers of the National Oceanic and Atmospheric Administration, merchant seamen with World War II service, and others

Restoration of Entitlement

Veterans can have previously-used entitlement "restored" to purchase another home with a VA loan if:

- The property purchased with the prior VA loan has been sold and the loan paid in full, or
- A qualified Veteran-transferee (buyer) agrees to assume the VA loan and substitute his or her entitlement for the same amount of entitlement originally used by the Veteran seller. The entitlement may be restored one time only if the Veteran has repaid

the prior VA loan in full, but has not disposed of the property purchased with the prior VA loan. Remaining entitlement and restoration of entitlement can be requested through the VA Eligibility Center by completing VA Form 26-1880.

Buying Process

In most cases, you need to follow these steps to get a VA home loan.

Eligibility Requirements for VA Home Loans

Find a real estate professional to work with. Perhaps a friend has someone to recommend or you could look under "Real Estate" in your yellow pages or on the Internet.

Find a Lender

Locate a lending institution that participates in the VA Home Loan program. You may want to get "pre-qualified" at this point – that is, find out how big of a loan that you can afford. Lenders set their own interest rates, discount points and closing points so you may want to shop around.

Get a Certificate of Eligibility

The Certificate of Eligibility (COE) verifies to the lender that you meet the eligibility requirements for a VA loan. See "Eligibility Requirements" above.

Find a Home and Sign a Purchase Agreement

Work with a real estate professional and negotiate a purchase agreement. Make sure the purchase and sales agreement contains a "VA Option Clause." Here is a sample of a "VA Option Clause":

"It is expressly agreed that, notwithstanding any other provisions of this contract, the purchaser shall not incur any penalty by forfeiture of earnest money or otherwise be obligated to complete the purchase of the property described herein, if the contract purchase price or cost exceeds the reasonable value of the property established by the Department of Veterans Affairs. The purchaser shall, however, have the privilege and option of proceeding with the consummation of this contract without regard to the amount of the reasonable value established by the Department of Veterans Affairs."

You may also want the purchase agreement to allow you to "escape" from the contract without penalty if you can't get a VA loan.

Apply for your VA Loan

Work with the lender to complete a loan application and gather the needed documents such as pay stubs and bank statements.

Loan Processing

The lender orders a VA appraisal and begins to "process" all the credit and income information. (Note: VA's appraisal is not a home inspection or a guarantee of value. It's just an estimate of the market value on the date of the inspection. Although the appraiser does look for obviously needed repairs, VA doesn't guarantee the condition of the house. The appraiser, who is licensed, in not a VA employee. The lender can't request a specific appraiser; assignments are made on a rotating basis.) The lending institution reviews the appraisal and all the documentation of credit, income and assets. The lender then decides whether the loan should be granted.

Closing

The lender chooses a title company, an attorney, or one of their own representatives to conduct the closing. This person will coordinate the date/time and the property is transferred. If you have any questions during the process that the lender can't answer to your satisfaction, please contact VA at your Regional Loan Center.

Loan Fee – VA Funding Fee

Generally, all Veterans using the VA Home Loan Guarantee benefit must pay a funding fee. This reduces the loan's cost to taxpayers considering that a VA loan requires no down payment and has no monthly mortgage insurance. The funding fee is a percentage of the loan amount which varies based on the type of loan and your military category, if you are a first-time or subsequent loan user, and whether you make a down payment. You have the option to finance the VA funding fee or pay it in cash, but the funding fee must be paid at closing time.

You do not have to pay the fee if you are a:

- Veteran receiving VA compensation for a service-connected disability, OR
- Veteran who would be entitled to receive compensation for a service-connected disability if you did not receive retirement or active duty pay, OR
- Surviving spouse of a Veteran who has died in service or from a service-connected disability

The funding fee for second time users who do not make a down payment is slightly higher. Also, National Guard and Reserve Veterans pay a slightly higher funding fee percentage. To determine your exact percentage, please review the latest funding fee chart.

Other Loan Costs

Be aware that the lender charges interest, in addition to closing fees and charges. Here are some general rules:

- The lender, not VA, sets the interest rate, discount points and closing costs. These rates may vary from lender to lender.

- Closing costs such as VA appraisal, credit report, state and local taxes, and recording feed may be paid by purchaser, the seller or shared.
- The seller can pay for some closing costs. (Under our rules, a seller's concessions can't exceed 4% of the loan. But only some types of costs fall under this 4% rule. Examples include: payment of pre-paid closing costs, VA funding fee, payoff of credit balances or judgments for the Veteran, and funds for temporary "buy-downs." Payment of discount points is not subject to the 4% limit.)
- You are not allowed to pay for the termite report, unless the loan is a refinance. That fee is usually paid by the seller.
- No commissions, brokerage fees, or "buyer broker" fees may be charged to the Veteran buyer.

Adding the VA Funding Fee and other loans costs to your loan may result in a situation in which you owe more than the fair market value of the house, and will reduce the benefit of refinancing since your payment will not be lowered as much as it could be. Also you could have difficulty selling the house for enough to pay off your loan balance.

Loan Limits

VA does not set a cap on how much you can borrow to finance your home. However, there are limits on the amount of liability VA can assume, which usually affects the amount of money an institution will lend you. The loan limits are the amount a qualified Veteran with full entitlement will lend you. The loan limits are the amount a qualified Veteran with full entitlement may be able to borrow without making a down payment. These loan limits may vary by county since the value of a house depends in part on its location.

The basic entitlement available to each eligible Veteran is $36,000. Lenders will generally loan up to 4 times a Veteran's available entitlement without a down payment, provided the Veteran is income and credit qualified and the property appraises for the asking price.

Remaining Entitlement

Veterans who had a VA loan before may still have "remaining entitlement" to use for another VA loan. Most lenders require that a combination of the guarantee entitlement and any cash down payment must equal at least 25% of the reasonable value or sales price of the property, whichever is less. Thus, for example, $23,000 remaining entitlement would probably meet a lender's minimum guarantee requirement for a no-down payment to buy a property valued at and selling for $94,000. You could also combine a down payment with the remaining entitlement for a larger loan amount.

Interest Rate Reduction Refinance Loan

The VA Interest Rate Reduction Refinance Loan (IRRRL) lowers your interest rate by refinancing your existing VA home loan. By obtaining a lower interest rate, your monthly mortgage payment should decrease. You can also refinance an adjustable rate mortgage (ARM) into a fixed rate mortgage.

IRRRL Facts

- No appraisal or credit underwriting is required when applying for an IRRRL.
- An IRRRL may be done with "no money out of pocket" by including all costs in the new loan or by making the new loan or by making the new loan at an interest rate high enough enable the lender to pay the costs.
- When refinancing from an existing VA ARM loan to a fixed rate loan, the interest rate may increase.
- No lender is required to give you an IRRRL, however, any VA lender of your choosing may process your application for an IRRRL.
- Veterans are strongly urged to contact several lenders because terms may vary.
- You may NOT receive any cash from the loan proceeds.

Eligibility

An IRRRL can only be made to finance a property on which you have already used you VA loan eligibility. It must be a VA to VA refinance, and it will reuse the entitlement you originally used.

Additionally:

- A Certificate of Eligibility (COE) is not required. If you have your Certificate of Eligibility, take it to the lender to show the prior use of your entitlement.
- No loan other than the existing VA loan may be paid from the proceeds of an IRRRL. If you have a second mortgage, the holder must agree to subordinate that lien so that your new VA loan will be a first mortgage.
- You may have used your entitlement by obtaining a VA loan when you brought your house, or by substituting your eligibility for that of the seller, if you assumed the loan.
- The occupancy requirement for an IRRRL is different from other VA loans. For an IRRRL you need only certify that you previously occupied the home.

Application Process

A new Certificate of Eligibility (COE) is not required. You may take your Certificate of Eligibility to show the prior use of your entitlement or your lender may use our e-mail confirmation procedure in lieu of a certificate of eligibility.

Note: Some lenders offer IRRRLs as an opportunity to reduce the term of your loan from 30 years to 15 years. While this can save you money in interest over the life of the loan, you may see a very large increase in your monthly payment if the reduction in interest rate is not at least one percent (two percent is better).

Beware: It could be a bigger increase than you can afford.

Housing Grants for Disabled Veterans

VA provides grants to service members and Veterans with certain permanent and total service-connected disabilities to help purchase or construct an adapted home, or modify an existing home to accommodate a disability. Two grant programs are available: the Specially Adapted Housing (SAH) grant and the Special Housing Adaption (SHA) grant.

Specially Adapted Housing (SAH) Grant

SAH grants help Veterans with certain service-connected disabilities live independently in a barrier free environment. SAH grants can be used in one of the following ways:

- Construct a specially adapted home on land to be acquired
- Build a home on land already owned if it is suitable for specially adapted housing
- Remodel an existing home if it can be made suitable for specially adapted housing
- Apply the grant against the unpaid principal mortgage balance of an adapted home already acquired without the assistance of a VA grant.

Special Housing Adaptation (SHA) Grant

SHA grants help Veterans with certain service-connected disabilities adapt or purchase a home to accommodate the disability. You can use SHA grants in one of the following ways:

- Adapt an existing home the Veteran or a family member already owns in which the Veteran lives.
- Adapt a home the Veteran or family member intends to purchase in which the Veteran will live
- Help a Veteran purchase a home already adapted in which the Veteran will live

Eligibility

If you are a service member or Veteran with a permanent and total service-connected disability, you may be entitled to a Specially Adapted Housing (SAH) grant or Special Housing Adaptation (SHA) grant. The tables below provide an overview of VA's housing grant programs for Veterans with certain service-connected disabilities.

Specially Adapted Housing (SAH) Grant

Eligibility	Living Situation	Ownership	Number of Grants You Can Use
Loss of or Loss of use of both legs, **OR**	Permanent	Home is owned by an eligible individual	Maximum of 3 grants, up to the maximum dollar amount allowable
Loss of or Loss of use of both arms, **OR**			
Blindness in both eyes having only light perception, plus loss of or loss of use of one leg, **OR**			
The loss of or Loss of use of one lower leg together with residuals of organic disease or injury, **OR**			
The loss of or Loss of use of one leg together with the loss of or loss of use of one arm, **OR**			
Certain severe burns, **OR**			
The loss of or Loss of use of one or more lower extremities due to service on or after September 11 2001, which so affects the functions of balance or propulsion as to preclude ambulating without the aid of braces, crutches, or a wheelchair.			

Special Housing Adaptation (SHA) Grant

Eligibility	Living Situation	Ownership	Number of Grants You Can Use
Blindness in both eyes with 20/200 visual acuity or less, **OR** Loss of or loss of use of both hands, **OR** Certain severe burn injuries, **OR** Certain severe respiratory injuries	Permanent	Home is owned by an eligible individual or family member	Maximum of 3 grants, up to the maximum dollar amount allowable

Benefit

The SAH and SHA benefit amount is set by law, but may be adjusted annually based on a cost-of-construction index. The maximum dollar amount allowable for SAH grants in fiscal year 2016 is $73,768. The maximum dollar amount allowable for SHA grant in fiscal year 2016 is $14,754. No individual may use the grant benefit more than three times up to the maximum dollar amount allowable.

A temporary grant may be available to SAH/SHA eligible Veterans and service members who are or will be temporarily residing in a home owned by a family member. The maximum amount available to adapt a family member's home for the SAH grant is $32,384 and for the SHA grant is $5,782.

How to Apply

To apply for a grant, fill out and submit VA Form 26-4555.

You can access this form by:

- Applying online via www.ebenefits.va.gov
- Mailing VA Form 26-4555 to your nearest VA Regional Loan Center (www.benefits.va.gov/HOMELOANS/contact_rlc_info.asp.)

- Calling VA toll free at 1-800-827-1000
- Visiting the nearest VA regional office

Mortgage Delinquency Assistance

In cases where loan servicers are unable to help Veteran borrowers, VA's Loan Guarantee Service has Loan Technicians in eight regional loan centers and a special servicing center who take an active role in interceding with the servicer to explore all options to avoid foreclosure. Service members or Veterans with VA-guaranteed home loans can call (877) 827-3702 to reach the nearest Loan Guarantee office where Loan Specialists are prepared to discuss potential ways to save the loan.

CHAPTER 13

Education and Training

Get Started

As a Veteran, you may be eligible for educational benefits through numerous GI Bill benefits it is important to choose the proper school and type of training. The VA's decision-making tools will help you get the most from your benefits.

CareerScope

In addition to Career Counseling, the Department of Veterans Affairs provides the interest and aptitude assessment tool known as CareerScope at no cost to all eligible benefit recipients. CareerScope has been used frequently by Veterans to determine the best career path for transition to civilian life.

Whether you wish to pursue education and training in a field you are already know, or wish to branch out to other fields that interest you, CareerScope can help. With CareerScope you will be provided with an assessment of your interests and aptitudes, and given recommendations about which careers you may enjoy and be successful doing, and what courses or training programs you should focus on to pursue those careers.

Education and Career Counseling Services

Free Educational and Career Counseling (Chapter 36) services are provided to transitioning service members who are:

- Within six months prior to discharge from active duty
- Within one year following discharge from active duty
- Current beneficiaries of educational assistance under Chapters 30, 31, 32, 33, 35, 1606, or 1607
- Veterans and qualifies dependents who are eligible for and have entitlement to educational assistance under Chapters 30, 31, 32, 33, 35, 1606, or 1607

Services Include:

- Counseling to facilitate career decision making for civilian or military occupations
- Educational and career counseling to choose an appropriate civilian occupation and develop a training program
- Academic and adjustment counseling to resolve barriers that impede success in training or employment

Comparison Tool/Payment Rates

You may be eligible for several types of VA education and training benefits, but there are many things to consider before you apply for a GI Bill program. For most participants, the Post 9/11 GI Bill is the best option. Other students would benefit more from the Montgomery GI Bill. The following comparison tools may make it easier to decide which education and training benefits are best for you:

1. The amount of time varies according to when the Veteran enlisted and entered active duty.
2. You may receive a maximum of 48 months of benefits combined if you are eligible for more than one VA education program.
3. Spouses are generally eligible to receive benefits for 10 years. However, spouses of individuals rated total and permanent within 3 years of discharge and spouses of individuals who die on active duty are granted a 20 year eligibility period.

	Post 9/11 GI Bill	MGIB-AD	MGIB-SR	REAP	VEAP	DEA
Minimum Length of Service	90 days active aggregate service (after 9/10/01) or 30 days continuous if discharged for disability	2 yr. continuous enlistment (minimum duty varies by service date, branch, etc.)	6 yr. commitment (after 6/30/85)	90 days active continuous service (after 9/10/01)	181 continuous days active service (between 12/31/76 and 7/1/85) (1)	Not Applicable N/A
Maximum # of Months of Benefits (2)	36	36	36	36	36	45
How Payments Are Made	Tuition: Paid to school Housing stipend: Paid monthly to student Books and Supplies: Paid to student at the beginning of the term	Paid to student	Paid to student	Paid to student	Paid to student	Paid to student

	Post 9/11 GI Bill	MGIB-AD	MGIB-SR	REAP	VEAP	DEA
Duration of Benefits	Generally 15 years from the last day of active duty	Generally 10 days from the last day of active duty	Ends the day you leave Selected Reserve	Generally 10 years from the day you leave the Selected Reserve or the day you leave the IRR (4)	10 years from last day of active duty	Spouse: 10 – 20 years (3) Child: Ages 18 – 26
Degree Training	Yes	Yes	Yes	Yes	Yes	Yes
Non-College Degree Training	Yes	Yes	Yes	Yes	Yes	Yes
On-the-Job and Apprenticeship Training	Yes	Yes	Yes	Yes	Yes	Yes
Flight Training	Yes	Yes	Yes	Yes	Yes	No
Correspondence Courses	Yes	Yes	Yes	Yes	Yes	Yes
Licensing and Certification	Yes	Yes	Yes	Yes	Yes	Yes
National Testing Programs	Yes	Yes	Yes	Yes	Yes	Yes
Work-Study Programs	Yes	Yes	Yes	Yes	Yes	Yes
Tutorial Assistance (5)	Yes	Yes	Yes	Yes	Yes	Yes

4. The Individual Ready Reserve (IRR) is a category of the Ready Reserve of the Reserve Component of the Armed Forces.
5. VA can pay the difference between the total cost of tuition and fees and the amount of Tuition Assistance paid by the military.

A Decision with Consequences

Your decision to apply for a certain education benefit could impact your eligibility for other benefits. Here are a few factors to keep in mind:

- If you are eligible for more than one education benefit, such as the Post 9/11 GI Bill and the Montgomery GI Bill, you must choose which benefit to receive, a decision that's final and cannot be changed.
- If you're eligible for the Post 9/11 GI Bill and two or more additional education benefits, you must give up one of the additional education benefits. However, you may remain eligible for the benefit or benefits you did not give up.

Apply for Benefits

Applying for your VA education benefits can be done in just a few steps:

- Apply online if you know which benefit you want to use.
- Visit your nearest VA regional office to apply in person.
- Consult with the VA Certifying Official – who is usually in the Registrar's or Financial Aid office – at the school of your choice. This official has application forms and can help you apply.
- Call 1-888-GI-BILL-1 (888-442-4551) to have the application mailed to you.

After you apply, use the VA's interactive map to find out how quickly your regional office is processing education claims. Your education benefits are processed at one of four specialized regional claims processing centers in Atlanta, GA; Buffalo, NY; Muskogee, OK; and St. Louis, MO.

Yellow Ribbon Program

The Post 9/11 GI Bill will pay you:

- All resident tuition and fees for a public school
- The lower of the actual tuition and fees or the national maximum per academic year for a private school.

Your actual tuition and fees costs may exceed these amounts if you are attending a private school or are attending a public school as a nonresident student. Institutions of Higher Learning (Degree Granting Institutions) may elect to participate in the Yellow Ribbon Program to make additional funds available for your education program without an additional charge to your GI Bill entitlement.

Degree-granted institutions of higher learning participating in the Post 9/11 GI Bill Yellow Ribbon Program agree to make additional funds available for your education program without an additional charge to your GI Bill entitlement. These institutions voluntarily enter into a Yellow Ribbon Agreement with VA and choose the amount of tuition and fees that will be contributed. VA matches that amount and issues payments directly to the institution.

Available Benefits and Eligibility

Only Veterans entitled to the maximum benefit rate, as determined by service requirements, or their designated transferees may receive this funding. Active duty service members and their spouses are not eligible for this program. Child transferees of active duty service members may be eligible if the service member is qualified at the 100 percent rate.

To receive benefits under the Yellow Ribbon Program:

- You must be eligible for the maximum benefit rate under the Post 9/11 GI Bill.
- You must not be on active duty or a spouse using transferred entitlement.
- Your school must agree to participate in the Yellow Ribbon Program.
- Your school must not have offered Yellow Ribbon to more than the maximum number of individuals, as stated in their participation agreement.
- Your school must certify your enrollment to the VA and provide Yellow Ribbon Program information.

You may be eligible if you fit the following circumstances:

- You served an aggregate period of 36 months in active duty after Sept. 10, 2001.
- You were honorably discharged from active duty for a service-connected disability and you served 30 continuous days after Sept. 10, 2001.
- You are a dependent eligible for Transfer of Entitlement under the Post 9/11 GI Bill based on the service eligibility criteria listed above.

CHAPTER 14

Vocational Rehabilitation and Employment

Transitioning to Civilian Employment

Vocational Rehabilitation and the Transition Assistance Program (TAP)

Explore your career options by attending a Transition Assistance Program (TAP) briefing. TAP is a joint effort by the Department of Defense, Department of Labor and Department of Veterans Affairs to inform service members and Veterans about many programs and services including Vocational Rehabilitation and the potentially life changing opportunities available. During the TAP briefing, there will be a component focusing on service for individuals with disabilities.

If you haven't already participated in a briefing, talk to your chain of command or call the Veterans Affairs at 1-800-827-1000 to be put in touch with a Vocational Rehabilitation Counselor.

Veteran Employment Tracks

Vocational Rehabilitation Counselors (VRC) and Employment Coordinators (EC) are ready to help Veterans and service members who have service-connected disabilities and an employment handicap find suitable careers. Your VRC will provide vocational counseling, refer you to appropriate opportunities and services specific to your needs, and help you reach your employment goals. If you are entitled to Vocational Rehabilitation and Employment benefits, you will work with a VRC to develop a personalized rehabilitation plan following one of five tracks:

Reemployment

When possible, Vocational Rehabilitation and Employment helps Veterans and service members return to work with a former employer by supporting the employer's efforts to provide accommodations that enable the Veteran to continue along the same or similar career path.

Rapid Access to Employment

Vocational Rehabilitation and Employment helps Veterans and service members who are ready to enter the workforce, find, apply for, and secure suitable jobs. The VA may provide professional job placement assistance, job accommodations, and other specialized support.

Self-employment

Self-employment can be fulfilling and may offer the flexibility a Veteran with service-connected disabilities needs. Vocational Rehabilitation and Employment can aid Veterans who are interested in working for themselves by helping analyze and develop a business plan, and providing training on how to market and operate a small business.

Employment Through Long-Term Services

For Veterans and service members who require additional skills or training to find competitive, suitable employment, Vocational Rehabilitation and Employment will provide assistance, which may include education benefits, on-the-job training, work-study, apprenticeships, or other job preparation programs to help them to obtain appropriate employment.

Independent Living

Some Veterans and service members may be unable to currently return to work, but with assistance from Vocational Rehabilitation and Employment, they can lead a more independent life. VA helps them with access to community-based support services, the use of assistive technologies and accommodations, and independent living skills training.

Veteran Employment Resources

The tools below can help you get prepared for the transition to your civilian career. Learn what to expect when you enter the job market and how to reflect your military skills on your resume, and then search for positions at VA's Veterans Employment Center jobs portal.

- Ten "Did You Know" Tips for Veterans Entering the Job Market
- How to Translate Your Military Occupational Specialty on Your Civilian Resume
- Veterans Employment Center

If you have a service-connected disability that makes it difficult for you to work in your previous profession, VA offers counseling, training, education, job placement, and other services to help you launch a new career. Find out if you are eligible and apply online at www.eBenefits.VA.gov.

Independent Living

Individuals whose service-connected disabilities require intensive and frequent rehabilitation supports may not be ready and able to work. When these individuals need help to become more independent in their homes and communities, the VA's Independent Living services can help them by providing assistance that may eventually enable them to pursue employment.

Each independent living plan is personalized to meet the individual's needs. In general, these services last up to 24 months, but services may be extended if certain criteria are met. Individuals who are pursuing employment goals may also receive independent living services when these services are needed to support the achievement of their vocational objective.

Independent Living Services may Include:

- Evaluation and counseling services to help determine independent living needs and identify goals
- Consultations with specialists such as physicians, physical therapists, occupational therapist, and rehabilitation engineers
- Information about and referral to resources such as health care services, special technology and equipment, community living support, and family counseling
- Information and assistance with exploring eligibility for home modification programs such as the Specially Adapted Housing (SAH) grant, and Home Improvements and Structural Alterations (HISA) grant
- Ongoing case support to help achieve independent living goals

Veterans Opportunity to Work (VOW)

Prepare for your next mission by accessing services you may have earned under the Veterans Opportunity to Work (VOW) program and other VA training and career assistance programs. Make your move from military to civilian life a success and get the training you need to thrive in your next career.

Transition Assistance Program

Transition GPS (Goals, Plans, Success)

The Transition Goals, Plans, Success program commonly known as Transition GPS was developed by the Department of Defense in coordination with the Department of Veteran Affairs and other partnering agencies. The program provides comprehensive services to our nation's service members to transition to work, life and home after the military.

Services You Have Earned

Transition GPS provides information about all of the benefits and services you've earned, and it goes way beyond job-search assistance. Here's just some of what the Transition GPS program offers:

- Pre-separation counseling: Before you exit the military, receive individual assessments and one-on-one counseling with military service representative experienced in the transition process.
- Enhanced VA benefits briefing: Learn about VA benefits during training sessions led by trained instructors covering the spectrum of what VA does to Veterans, service members, family members, and survivors.

You will receive information on these and other benefits to assist you through transition:

- Education and employment programs to bolster your job skills and kick-start your career
- VA benefits and services to improve your overall quality of life
- Other benefits to assist in building and maintaining a stable home environment

Plans Designed for You

The Transition GPS program is designed to make your post-military adjustment easier. All transitioning service members are required to take part in the program including Guard and reserve members demobilizing after 180 days or more of active service (Title 10).

Make your transition a success with these services:

- Individual Transition Planning: What are your skills, what jobs interest you, and what's next? A customized roadmap will help you outline and achieve your career goals.
- Employment Workshop: What are civilian employers looking for from job applicants? During the sessions, employment specialists will help you translate your military skills into civilian employment, search for a job, write an effective resume, and interview successfully.
- Tailored Tracks: Three optional workshops: Career Technical Training Track, Education Track, and Entrepreneurship Track are also available through Transition GPS. Service members can elect to attend one or all three in preparation for separation or retirement.

Part of VA's role within Transition GPS is instructing the Career Technical Training Track. This course guides service members, military spouses, and Veterans through a variety of decisions involved in identifying a technical career, determining credentials requirements, researching and applying to training programs, exploring funding options, and creating a plan for success. After completing this program, participants will be prepared to develop a customized plan for a successful transition into a technical career.

How You'll Learn

Through two briefings, VA Benefits I and II, you will learn what you need to know about VA benefits and services in a highly interactive, activity-based class attended by your peers. Information is provided through these briefings:

VA Benefits I: This is a four-hour briefing providing information on education, health care, compensation, life insurance, and home loans, as well as vocational rehabilitation and employment benefits information and counseling. The program assists you in developing a personal plan of action for using VA benefits. It's open to 50 attendees per class. Spouses and family members are encouraged to attend.

VA Benefits II: This two-hour supplemental briefing with video presentations provides an overview of the eBenefits portal and further information on VA health care benefits and services and the disability compensation process. Valuable guidance is provided on benefit options and how to navigate eBenefits.va.gov.

Eligibility and Entitlement

Services that may be provided by the Vocational Rehabilitation and Employment Program include:

- Comprehensive evaluation to determine abilities, skills, and interests for employment
- Vocational counseling and rehabilitation planning for employment services
- Employment services such as job-training, job seeking skills, resume development, and other work readiness assistance
- Assistance finding and keeping a job, including the use of special employer incentives and job accommodations
- On the Job Training (OJT), apprenticeships, and non-paid work experiences
- Post-secondary training at a college, vocational, technical or business school
- Supportive rehabilitation services including case management, counseling, and medical referrals

- Independent living services for Veterans unable to work due to the severity of their disabilities

Active Duty Service Members are Eligible if They:

- Expect to receive an honorable or other than dishonorable discharge upon separation from active duty
- Obtain a memorandum rating of 20 percent or more from the Department of Veterans Affairs (VA)
- Apply for Vocational Rehabilitation and Employment services

Veterans are Eligible if They:

- Have received, or will receive, a discharge that is other than dishonorable
- Have a service-connected disability of at least 10 percent from VA
- Apply for Vocational Rehabilitation and Employment services

Basic Period of Eligibility

The basic period of eligibility ends 12 years from the date of notification of one of the following:

- Date of separation from active military service.
- Date the veteran was first notified by VA of a service-connected disability rating.

The basic period of eligibility may be extended if a Vocational Rehabilitation Counselor (VRC) determines that a Veteran has a Serious Employment Handicap (SEH) which is considered to be a significant impairment of a Veteran or service member's ability to prepare for, obtain, or retain employment consistent with his or her abilities, aptitudes, and interests. The SHE must result in substantial part from a service-connected disability. For Veterans rated at 10 percent and Veterans beyond their 12-year basic period of eligibility, the finding of a SEH is necessary to establish entitlement to Vocational Rehabilitation and Employment services.

What Happens after Eligibility is Established?

The Veteran is scheduled to meet with a VRC for a comprehensive evaluation to determine if he/she is entitled by services. A comprehensive evaluation includes:

- An assessment of the Veteran's interests, aptitudes and abilities
- An assessment of whether service connected disabilities impair the Veteran's ability to find and/or hold a job using the occupational skills he or she has already developed
- Vocational exploration and goal development leading to employment and/or maximum independence at home and in the Veteran's community

What is an Entitlement Determination?

A VRC works with the Veteran to complete a determination if an employment handicap exists. An employment handicap exists if the Veteran's service connected disability impairs his/her ability to obtain and maintain a job. Entitlement to services is established if the veteran has an employment handicap and is within his or her 12-year basic period of eligibility and has a 20% or greater service-connected disability rating.

If the service-connected disability rating is less than 20% or if the Veteran is beyond the 12-year basic period of eligibility, then a serious employment handicap must be found to establish entitlement to Vocational Rehabilitation and Employment services. A serious employment handicap is based on the extent of services required to help a Veteran overcome his or her service and non-service connected disabilities permitting the return to suitable employment.

What Happens After the Entitlement Determination is Made?

- Determine transferable skills, aptitudes and interests
- Identify viable employment and/or independent living service options
- Explore labor market and wage information
- Identify physical demands and other job characteristics
- Narrow vocational options to identify a suitable employment goal
- Select a Vocational Rehabilitation and Employment program track leading to an employment or independent living goal
- Investigate training requirements
- Identify resources needed to achieve rehabilitation
- Develop an Individualized Written Rehabilitation Plan (IWRP) to achieve the identified employment and or independent living goals

What is a Rehabilitation Plan?

A rehabilitation plan is an individualized, written outline of the services, resources and criteria that will be used to achieve employment and/or independent living goals. The plan is an agreement that is signed by the Veteran and the VRC and is updated as needed to assist the Veteran in achieving his/her goals. Depending on their circumstances, veterans will work with their VRC to select one or more of the following five tracks of services:

- Reemployment (with a former employer)
- Direct job placement services for new employment
- Self-employment
- Employment through long term services including OJT, college and other training
- Independent living services

What Happens after the Rehabilitation Plan is Developed?

After a plan is developed and signed, a VRC or case manager will continue to work with the Veteran to implement the plan to obtain suitable employment and/or independent living. The VRC or case manager will provide ongoing counseling, assistance, and coordinate services such as tutorial assistance, training in job-seeking skills, medical and dental referrals, adjustment counseling, payment of training allowance, if applicable, and other services as required to help the Veteran achieve rehabilitation.

How can I get paid the Post 9/11 GI Bill rate for my Vocational Rehabilitation Program?

A Veteran participating in the Vocational Rehabilitation and Employment Program who qualifies for Post 9/11 GI Bill benefits can elect to receive the GI Bill rate of pay instead of the regular Chapter 31 subsistence allowance. In most cases, the GI Bill rate is higher than the regular Chapter 31 rate of pay. To elect the GI Bill rate, the Veteran must have remaining eligibility for the Post 9/11 GI Bill, and must formally choose (or "elect") the GI Bill rate. Your VRC can help you with the election.

Veterans participating in the Vocational Rehabilitation and Employment Program who elect the Post 9/11 rate are paid at the 100% rate for their school and training time, even if their Post 9/11 GI Bill eligibility is less than 100%. Additional benefits are also available through the Vocational Rehabilitation and Employment program, such as full payment of all books, fees and supplies as well as other supportive services.

CHAPTER 15

What Do I Want to Do With My Life?

SOMETIMES IF YOU ARE NOT certain how to proceed it can be helpful to to figure out where you want to end up. Having determined where you want to go you can then work backwards to where you are. As an example, while looking at careers you discover that some of the highest entry level salaries are in Science, Technology, Engineering and Math and these are commonly referred to as STEM fields.

You know you are interested in technology, and did okay in a chemistry class you took using Tuition Assistance. You start reading and come across a job description of a Biomedical Engineer. According to the Bureau of Labor Statistics a Biomedical Engineer analyzes and designs a solution to problems in biology and medicine, with the goal of improving the quality and effectiveness of patient care.

You start reading and think why can't I do that? The fact is you can. I am not going to say that it will be easy. There will be times when you want to just walk away and say forget it. Having served in the armed forces, you have been placed in difficult and stressful situations. You did not quit then and if this is really what you want to do, you will not quit now.

So you need figure out what you need to do to get a job as a Biomedical Engineer. According to our friends at the Bureau of Labor Statistics (BLS), Biomedical Engineers typically need a bachelor's degree in Biomedical Engineering from an accredited program to enter the occupation. Alternatively, they need a bachelor's degree in a different field of engineering and then get a graduate degree in biomedical engineering or get on-the-job training in biomedical engineering.

So now we know that you have to go get an engineering degree from an accredited engineering program. So how do you identify what an accredited engineering program is and which schools have them? According to the BLS, Biomedical Engineering programs are accredited by the Accreditation Board for Engineering and Technology (ABET). A simple google search (try – abet accredited biomedical engineering schools) will provide a list that you can start with. Let's say you live in Pittsburgh. Fortunately, the University of Pittsburgh has an accredited program.

A quick look at the University of Pittsburgh's website shows you can complete an undergraduate degree in Bioengineering by enrolling as a Freshman or as a Transfer Student. It would be a good idea to take a tour of the school and talk to students as well as faculty members and administrators. It would also be wise to see what resources are available for veterans. Having researched the school and understood the requirements for acceptance, the question you need to ask is, have you completed the coursework necessary to be accepted to the program.

If you have not completed the necessary coursework or do not have the grades to be accepted, you may want to take some classes at a junior or community college. If you decide to do this, make sure that any classes that you do take will transfer and that the classes fit within your curriculum degree plan. The best way to accomplish this is to speak with the staff at the school and see what they recommend.

Once you have a plan regarding what classes you need to take, you can enroll and begin your studies. That brings us to the next question that you need to figure out before you enroll. How am I going to pay for this?

Paying for School

As an active duty service member or as a veteran, there are programs that can help you pay for school. There are scholarships that are specifically targeted for those who have and do serve. There is the GI Bill (Montgomery or Post 9/11) and Educational Benefits offered through the Veterans Administration (VA). There is merit-based and need-based aid. There are also loans, but loans should be used as a last resort and used sparingly. You have served your country, with a lot of hard work and a little luck, you should be able to graduate from college without relying on loans to finance the bulk of your undergraduate education.

Transitioning from Military Life to a Life in the Classroom

Fact: You are going to be older than most of your classmates. Fact: You have a lifetime of experience that they cannot imagine. Fact: You will be much more serious about you studies than the vast majority of your classmates. Fact: They will always ask why you are so rigid, formal, and/ or serious.

Older students have difficulty relating to students that are straight out of high school. For many of them, this is the first time they have lived away from their families. To you, they may seem unfocused and undisciplined. They have no respect for time or punctuality and have no sense of urgency. You will find yourself annoyed by a lot of what you see. Learn to live with it. Try to find adult learners. Try to find other veterans who may be experiencing what you are.

Try to find organizations that resonate with you and may help you integrate with your younger peers. Take advantage of the career center on campus. This should be your opportunity to shine. You can strengthen areas where you are weak and learn how to deal with people who are much younger than you, this skill will be invaluable for future interactions in the workplace.

Cooperative Education and Internships are golden opportunities. You have life and work experience. You have the focus, maturity and discipline that employers crave. You have the opportunity to gain experience that when combined with your military background will allow you to enter the workplace far ahead of your peers. You have worked hard to have this chance. Make sure that you seize it, but don't forget to take the time to enjoy and explore areas that challenge your preconceptions.

I Don't want to Go to a Traditional Four Year School

There are those who may not want to go to a four-year school. The fact is that there is nothing wrong with that. Some people like to work with their hands and everyone does not want or need an Undergraduate Degree. You can make a great living as a skilled tradesman (Plumber, Auto Repair Technician, Electrician, etc.) without having to attend a traditional college. You can also pursue and find work in occupations that require an Associates Degree or Certificate Programs (i.e. Information Technology: Network Engineering).

If you are eligible, an alternative to utilizing your GI Bill benefits is Vocational Rehabilitation. This program is a better fit for some veterans as it can be tailored more towards the needs of the veteran. The purpose of the program is to determine and provide a veteran with the skills, experience and opportunity to live independently and obtain work or start a business. A veteran is matched with a counselor and the counselor and veteran work together to find what best matches the aptitude and capability of the veteran with the goal of enabling the veteran to be self-sufficient.

How do I Make Employers Understand My Value?

There is no simple answer to that question. Everyone is not a great communicator. If this is not a skill that comes naturally to you, it is something that you just have to practice. Understand that you have to be aware of your audience. You need to be aware of who you are speaking to. The language you may use when you are among close friends is not the language you want to use when you are in an interview. You need to practice by talking about yourself, talking about what you have done, what you have learned and the impact you have had in accomplishing personal and/or team goals.

You need to be able to take your personal experiences and relate it to what the employer does. Let's say you were a mechanic and drove heavy machinery in the military. You are interviewing with a company for a job as a heavy equipment operator where you would operate bulldozers, skid steers, front-end loaders and excavators. Being able to relate what you have done in the military demonstrates that you have experience operating and maintaining heavy equipment. It demonstrates that you know how to be responsible and are punctual. It demonstrates that you know how to finish what you start. These are all things that an employer wants.

The skills that you have accumulated during your service distinguish you from other applicants. You have demonstrated the ability to adapt to changing conditions and know how to deal with pressure and deadlines. You have experience dealing with equipment worth millions of dollars. You understand the chain of command and when you are given an assignment you get it done. You need to make sure employers understand this.

Bearing and Communication

You may have heard someone say that it is not what you know but who you know that decides if you succeed or not. I have found that's not exactly true. My experience has taught me that while who you know is important, it is not as important as who knows YOU. People tend to go out of their way for people they know and people they like. For the most part, people only do what is required in the performance of their duties. That being said, people tend to go above and beyond what is required when we have a connection to the person we are dealing with.

The manner in which you carry yourself speaks louder than anything you will ever say. As a veteran, you stand apart from your peers due to your posture, your discipline, and your character. This is an asset that you can use to open doors that are closed to most people. To do this you will need to develop what I call soft skills.

The ability to be a mechanic, to play an instrument, or throw a football are physical tangible skills. You use your physical senses to feel and touch. Soft skills are more intangible. Soft skills allow you to relate to people and communicate more effectively. They allow you to understand what someone is going through, and to provide a solution to a problem they do not realize they have. Soft skills are an indication of your leadership capacity, the ability to recognize that different people are motivated by different things. The key is recognizing what motivates the people you are dealing with adjusting your approach to dealing with them.

An interview is a perfect example of this. When you walk into the interview, you believe that you are the one being interviewed. This is true, but what you may not realize is that you are also interviewing the company that is holding the interview. The interview is an opportunity for you to learn more about the position, the company and to make a determination regarding how you may fit in the company climate.

If you do not realize this and fail to take advantage, you are missing a golden opportunity. The interview is where you can show off the research that you have done and ask the type of probing questions that provide the interviewer insight regarding your thought process. They can see that you have taken the interview seriously and that you are a professional in all things.

Recruiters review countless resumes and interview multiple candidates for positions. Making the cut and being granted an interview is an indication of how highly they thought of you. This is your opportunity to stand out from everyone else they are interviewing. You have an opportunity to share a little about yourself, and your background. You have a chance to explain how the combination of your education, skills and your military service distinguish you from others in the applicant pool. Make sure you take advantage of this.

Cultivating a Network

One of the most important resources a professional has is their network of friends, associates and colleagues. Everyone you come across is a potential network contact. It is up to you to meet, develop and maintain these relationships. Getting involved in professional associations, social organizations or charitable pursuits is a great way to meet people you normally do not associate with. As you volunteer your time, you may find you interact with many potential contacts that may be of use to you as you navigate your career.

You have to understand that this is a two-way street as well. You may be called upon to provide assistance to someone else. Sometimes being of service to others leads to someone recommending you to someone that will be a useful contact later on. Doing things because it is the right thing to do and doing so without expecting anything in return, speaks volumes about your character and is noticed even if you are not aware of it.

It is not enough to just make contacts. As uncomfortable as it may be you have to do the hard work of maintaining these contacts. I understand that veterans are not always the most open and social people. Some of us can be quite the curmudgeon, but we have a bond earned through service that people who have not served do not understand. If you have the time and resources to share with a veteran, you should do it because you may have needed someone at one point and you understand how it feels to be in a similar situation.

I Have Graduated... So Now What Do I Do?

All of our lives we have been told in order to be successful you need an education. We have been told to be responsible, go to school, and get a good job. Congratulations, all the hard work you have done has earned you a diploma. Hopefully, you have followed the advice regarding Internships, Co-Operative Education and developing your soft skills. If you are lucky, you have a job offer or hopefully offers (plural) in hand. Unfortunately, everyone does not have a job lined up when they graduate and have to make some decisions regarding what to do.

The major that you have chosen combined with the work experience you have obtained have a great deal to do with how difficult it may be for you to find a job to support yourself and your obligations. This is where your network can be of tremendous assistance. The career center at school, professors, fellow students, hell even the guy who cuts the grass can be of assistance. Anyone that can help you find a job needs to be on your radar. Now is not the time to be too proud to reach out for help.

As a veteran, you are probably eligible for Veterans Preference when it comes to applying for a job with the Federal Government. Finding and obtaining a Federal position can be a long and arduous task but the time you served in the military can be counted in when calculating the length of your total federal service for retirement purposes.

You can also explore looking for work as a Federal Contractor. Working as a contractor has positive and negative characteristics that you have to weigh when making a decision as to whether being a contractor is a good fit for your life:

Issue 1: You are a Contract Worker

As a contract worker your contract can be cancelled or not renewed. This means that your job may go away and you need to find a new contract. The contractor you are working for may place you on another contract, but that is not guaranteed. You are playing by a different set of rules than the government employees you may be working side by side with.

Issue 2: You Pay Your Own Taxes, Healthcare and Retirement

As a contractor, you are paid a salary that seems large but out of that salary you are responsible for paying your own taxes. You are the recipient of a 1099 and you pay your taxes quarterly. You are responsible for paying for your own healthcare and are responsible for funding your own retirement. If you don't plan and save accordingly, you may experience financial difficulties.

You may decide that you do not want to get a job working for someone and decide to launch your own venture. You may decide to start your own business or even look into franchising. The point is that there are a wealth of opportunities that you can explore in trying to determine what will be the best fit for you, your family and your long term goals. Understand that you are going to change jobs over the course of your career and that where you begin will definitely not be the point where you end.

CHAPTER 16

The Lesson

SO HAVING READ ALL OF this let's review what have we we learned. You should go into a life in the military knowing that it will end. Armed with this knowledge, you need to begin planning an exit strategy on the first day your military career begins. You need to build a foundation of sound financial habits because these habits will stay with you for the rest of your life. You need to invest in strengthening your mind and your personal relationships.

Learning how to effectively communicate and being honest about expectations in both your personal and professional life can save you time, energy and money. Being open to lifelong learning and acting on opportunities when they present themselves will be critical in continuing to acquire the skills and relationships that will sustain you over your life.

Remember it is okay if you make a mistake. The important thing to realize is that we often learn more from the mistakes that we make than if we had just done everything right the first time. Conquering adversity teaches you how to get up after being knocked down. It is easy to complain about what you do not have, and what someone else does have. It is much harder to do something about it. There will always be someone telling you what you cannot do. Truly successful people are so busy doing what someone said they cannot do to hear them say it.

Made in the USA
Middletown, DE
15 May 2016